THE
REINCARNATION
SENSATION

THE
REINCARNATION
SENSATION

Norman L. Geisler
& J. Yutaka Amano

Tyndale House Publishers, Inc.
Wheaton, Illinois

All Scripture quotations
are taken from the
New American Standard Bible.

First printing, November 1986
Library of Congress
Catalog Card Number
86-51091
ISBN 0-8423-5404-2
Copyright 1986
by Norman L. Geisler
and J. Yutaka Amano

CONTENTS

CHAPTER 1
POPULARITY OF REINCARNATION

Move backward in time. . . . Together, we are going to journey backward in time to one of your *previous lifetimes*. . . . A lifetime that will be of value for you to recall will be chosen by your subconscious. . . .

I want you to create a mental picture of a tunnel. It is a tunnel to your own past. As I begin to count backwards from five to one, you will see yourself moving through your tunnel and into your past. . . .

Step into the tunnel. Number five. You've begun your journey now. Four. Feel yourself moving backward into your own past. Three. At the end of the tunnel, you see a light. Move towards that light. Two. Let yourself go. On the count of one you'll be able to see where you've lived, touch what you have held, know who you have been, you will be . . . there. One. . . .[1]

See also p 37

—David Yarborough

According to a 1982 Gallup poll, 23 percent of Americans, that is, almost one in every four, believes in reincarnation.[2] This is so even though nine out of every ten Americans claim Christianity as their religious preference.[3] This proportion increases to 30 percent among college-age persons—eighteen to twenty-four years old. Furthermore, about 17 percent of those who claim to attend church regularly also claim to believe in reincarnation. The figures are even more astonishing when one is confronted with statistics that claim that 21 percent of the Protestant population and 25 percent of professing Catholics believe in reincarnation.

HOW POPULAR IS THE BELIEF IN REINCARNATION?

The popularity of the belief in reincarnation is not only evidenced by the Gallup poll percentages but also by the many famous advocates of this Eastern doctrine. One of the most popular proponents in recent times is actress, dancer-singer, and author Shirley MacLaine.

SHIRLEY MACLAINE

It would be little exaggeration to call 1984 the "Year of MacLaine." With an estimated net worth of more than $15 million, she won an Academy Award for best actress in April 1984 for her part as Aurora Greenway in *Terms of Endearment.* In addition, she grossed a record $475,000 per week at the 1,992-seat Gershwin Theater for her show *Shirley MacLaine on Broadway* and was given the prominent cover story position of the May 14th, 1984, issue of *Time* magazine.

Not least of these accomplishments is the phenomenal popularity of her new book *Out on a Limb*, which has been in the top spot on the *New York Times* paperback best-seller list, 176,000 copies having been printed in hardcover and about 1.2 million in paperback. She describes this book as

8

the experience of getting in touch with myself. . . . And what I learned as a result has enabled me to get on with the rest of my life as an almost transformed human being.

So this book is a quest for self—a quest which took me on a long journey that was gradually revealing and at all times simply amazing. I tried to keep an open mind as I went because I found myself gently but firmly exposed to dimensions of time and space that heretofore, for me, belonged in science fiction or what I would describe as the occult.[4]

This "quest for self" is really what she calls her "inner journey" into her past lives. In fact, the title of the *Time* magazine article on her was "The Best Year of Her *Lives*" (emphasis added). Although she came from a Christian background, the concept of reincarnation "seemed like a good dimension to explore."

MacLaine said, "I know that *I* must have been many different people in many different times." She has claimed to be " 'a former prostitute, my own daughter's daughter, and a male court jester who was beheaded by Louis XV of France'—all in past incarnations that she believes she has rediscovered with the aid of mediums, meditation and, in at least one case, acupuncture."[5] As she was decapitated by Louis XV for telling "impertinent jokes," MacLaine recalls, "I watched my head rolling on the floor. . . . It landed face up, and a big tear came out of one eye."[6] She also "remembered very clearly the feeling of living in Atlantis. . . . I was a man, a great teacher, very much in love with my wife, . . . I couldn't stand the thought of drowning, so I killed myself."[7]

Near her California retreat, she attended an "ashram" in 1974 at the cost of $1,300 for six days. An ashram is a "hermitage," an open monastery or retreat center which is used for meditation and self-discipline. There she was trained in "hatha-yoga." Hatha is Sanskrit for "force" and yoga means "yoke" or "union." Thus, hatha-yoga refers to the discipline which stresses posture, exercises, breath control, and meditation in order to align one's "force" with "the universal Force." It is a practical means for the individual self to attain union with the "universal soul."

MacLaine claims that the ashram has been a catalyst in her belief in "karmic consciousness" and reincarnation. While costars Jack Nicholson and Debra Winger were giving interviews in Hollywood to promote the film *Terms of Endearment* in November 1983, MacLaine was sleeping in the pyramids of Egypt in search of her former selves.[8]

This search has led MacLaine to a missionary-type vision of spreading her belief in reincarnation. This is why she titled her book *Out on a Limb*. To go "out on a limb" is to risk embarrassment in the proclamation of the gospel of reincarnation. Her mentor told her, "You can help others understand God through themselves by sharing the account of how you understand God through *yourself*." MacLaine's sequel to her best-seller, *Dancing in the Light*, further explores her belief in reincarnation. However, this book looks deeper into the occultic aspect of Eastern mysticism.

OTHER CELEBRITIES

Peter Sellers, of the "Pink Panther" fame and many other zany characters, confided in MacLaine his belief in reincarnation. In fact, he believed that the reason why he could perform his impersonations so well was because "he had *been* those characters at one time in a way that could only be described as 'having lived them in the past.' "[9]

A year and half later, when MacLaine was told by a reporter that Peter Sellers had died, she said, "I could feel

Peter watching me. I wanted to tell the reporter he was mistaken. I wanted to say, 'Yes, you probably *think* he's dead, but he's really only left his latest body.' "

Paddy Chayevsky is the author of the novel-turned-motion picture *Altered States*. This story is about a scientific genius, Eddie Jessup, who experiments with a sensory isolation tank. Inside the tank he is entirely isolated from sight and sound, experiencing "sensory deprivation." As he floats alone in an Epsom salt solution, his heartbeat and breathing cause his body to move erratically. Added to the feeling of weightlessness, this whole process creates an altered state of consciousness that can produce out-of-body experiences and induce psychic powers. As Dr. Jessup experiments with the tank and a mind-altering drug, he experiences creation in reverse.

Before Chayevsky died, he told MacLaine that he had done extensive scientific research on his novel and believed "that every human being carries, locked in his or her cellular memory, the entire experience of the human race from the beginning of creation." This idea assumes that one has a collection of conscious memories of past lives and events from which one could draw upon.

"Heavyweight" Hollywood star Sylvestor "Rocky" Stallone was supposedly once beheaded by the Jacobins in the French Revolution. He claims to have been an American Indian, a monkey in Guatemala, and a wolf. Unsurprisingly, Stallone told *Time* reporter John Leo that he "wants to come back some day as a heavyweight boxing champion."[10]

Country singer Loretta Lynn believed herself to be the product of at least six reincarnations. She was a Cherokee princess, an Irish woman, a rural American housewife, the wife of a bedridden old man, a 1920s male restaurant employee, and a roving maid for one of the King Georges of England.[11]

Other Hollywood believers in reincarnation include Glenn Ford, Glenn Scarpelli *(One Day at a Time)*, Lee Cureri *(Fame)*, Audrey Landers *(Dallas)*, and Anne Francis *(Honey West, Funny Girl, Forbidden Planet)*. Anne Francis believes that she has lived many lives before, but one that would shock most of us is her declaration, *"I* was Mary Magdalene's mother!"[12]

General George S. Patton, commander of U.S. forces in North Africa, Sicily, and the invasion of Europe which led to Hitler's defeat, saw himself as a reincarnation of one of Napoleon's generals, a legion commander in Caesar's army, and a leader who fought beside Richard the Lion-Hearted in the Third Crusade.[13]

Henry Ford, the automobile industrialist, in a 1928 interview in the *San Francisco Examiner,* claimed to have adopted the theory of reincarnation when he was twenty-six years old, seeing his genius as "the fruit of long experience in many lives."

The great Spanish painter Salvador Dali believed he was a reincarnation of the Spanish mystic, St. John of the Cross.

The American author and humorist Mark Twain recalled his acquaintance with the Greek philosopher Socrates as they lounged in a house of Athens.

COMIC BOOKS

Reincarnation has also recently been the dominant theme of many popular comic books. *Camelot 3000* is a special twelve-issue maxi-series, published by DC Comics, Inc., which began in December 1982. This company, which has published such comic book favorites as Superman, Wonderwoman, and Batman, begins this tale with the legendary King Arthur being awakened from an ancient tomb by a young man in the year 3000 when Earth is being invaded by monstrous aliens. King Arthur then travels to Stonehenge where he invokes his old mentor, "Merlin, Son of the Devil," to come to his aid. Together they are magically transported to a nuclear plant where Merlin conjures up the Lady of the Lake so that King Arthur can retrieve Excalibur.

But the magical sword is not all that the King of Camelot retrieves. In the course of time, Arthur is reunited with his fellow knights, Lancelot, Percival, and Galahad. He is also reunited with his queen, Guinevere. In conversation with the king, Merlin explains she "did not 'sleep' all this time, Arthur. She is a *reincarnate*—her *soul* has been reborn in another *body!*"

Sir Tristan, who once served on Arthur's round table, regretfully comes back as a woman. And later, Sir Tristan, frustrated with himself (herself?) because he/she needed the help of another in order to destroy an enemy, says: "I'm *not* a woman! I'm a *man*. . . . I just have the *body* of a woman!"

It was inevitable that Sir Tristan meet Isolde, the reincarnation of his girlfriend in old Camelot. Refusing to believe she is Isolde, Tristan is finally convinced when she kisses him/her. Thus, the encounter involves two women kissing each other. Repulsed, Tristan tears himself/herself away from Isolde and agonizes: "Was I so *evil* in my first life? What did I do to deserve *this?*" In a later issue, Tristan cries out, "I'm not supposed to *be* a woman, milady! This—female body results from an unfortunate mistake in my *reincarnation.*"

A further complication arises when the reincarnated Lancelot and Guinevere once again commit adultery and betray Arthur.

Arthur then sums up the tragedy of "reincarnating" past mistakes: "How could you *do* this? To *me,* to the *table round* . . . How could you do this *again?* Throughout all *time,* men have longed for *nothing* so much as a *second* chance. You were *given* such a chance . . . and you *failed.*"

Ronin is another comic book series that has as one of its main themes the subject of reincarnation. This series is about an ancient samurai warrior who calls himself Ronin, who made a vow to avenge his master Lord Ozaki from the "shapechanger, the demon . . . Agat" *(Ronin,* July 1983). He is reincarnated into the future in the form of a limbless Billy Challas, someone who is psychokinetically connected to powerful mechanical limbs. "Magic," supposedly from the soul of Ronin, literally constructs a cybernetic body out of Billy, thus housing the reincarnated soul of Ronin.

Another popular comic magazine, *Doctor Strange, Master of the Mystic Arts* (i.e., the occult), published by Marvel Comics Group, dealt with reincarnation in its August 1984 issue. In this story, three monks from the Far East ask Dr. Strange to help them in their search for their High Lama's reincarnated self.

The belief in reincarnation is getting to be so popular that Past-Life Therapist Dick Sutphen, who formed Reincarnationists, Inc., in 1982, wants to build a Reincarnationist Spiritualist Center in the "energy vortex area of Sedona, Arizona." This center will be used for research, media communications, and seminars. Sedona has been picked as the best site for this venture because "the phenomenal positive psychic energy of this location will expand our own communication energy and assure far greater results than we could achieve elsewhere."[14]

WHY IS THE BELIEF IN REINCARNATION SO POPULAR?

The meteoric rise in popularity of the belief in reincarnation leads us properly to ask why this is so. Several possible reasons for this surge of interest will be presented in the rest of this chapter.

THE TURN EAST

In the *Doctor Strange* issue on reincarnation, Dr. Strange discovers that the high priest has been reincarnated as a blonde-haired, blue-eyed Caucasian. One of the monks then attempts to correct what he perceives as "a single error of reincarnation" because their great high priest has been exposed to the decadence of the material world. The monk says, "Your body must die that the Lama may be born again, purging this horrible experience from his karma."

Dr. Strange must then rescue the Lama from the misguided monk's murderous assault. The blue-eyed Lama then mercifully explains to his mistaken disciple: "My incarnation here was not some mystical mistake. . . . So much has happened to the world in this century . . . *east and west grow closer every day.* It was necessary that I be reborn in America" (emphasis added).

Whether the publishers of this magazine realized it or not, they stumbled upon one of the most significant ideological movements in America at this time. The West is, as Harvard Divinity School professor Harvey Cox titled his book, *Turning East.* In this work, Professor Cox writes:

> The influence of Oriental spirituality in the West is hardly something new.
>
> But there is something new about the present situation. In previous decades, interest in Oriental philosophy was confined mostly to intellectuals and was centered largely on ideas, not on devotional practices. . . . Today, on the other hand, not only are large numbers of people who are in no sense "intellectuals" involved, but they appear more interested in actual

religious practices than in doctrinal ideas. The recent wave of spirituality seems both broader and deeper than the ones that preceded it.

> . . . the fact is that large numbers of people are involved, not just a fringe group, and the extent of the interest has no precedent in American religious history.[15]

A friend and colleague of the late Francis Schaeffer, Os Guinness, wrote in his highly touted work, *The Dust of Death:*

> The point is this: The East is still the East, but the West is no longer the West. Western answers no longer seem to fit the questions. With Christian culture disintegrating and humanism failing to provide an alternative, many are searching the ancient East.[16]

Even social forecaster John Naisbitt in his best-seller, *Megatrends,* noted "the widespread interest in Eastern religions"[17] since the 1960s.

The most spectacular trilogy of movie history, *Star Wars, The Empire Strikes Back,* and *The Return of the Jedi,* has recently been exposed as latent with an Eastern worldview. George Lucas, the creative genius behind this *Star Wars* phenomena, looks at his films as "a modern morality play, a psychological tool that children can use to understand the world better and their place in it and how to adjust to that."[18]

In Lucas's biography, *Skywalking,* Dale Pollock discovered that "Lucas's concept of the Force was heavily influenced by Carlos Castaneda's *Tales of Power.* This is an account of a Mexican Indian sorcerer, Don Juan, who uses the phrase 'life force.' "[19] Lucas's "religion of the Force" was derived from Castaneda's writings which were based on Eastern beliefs. Ordained Hindu monk Agehananda Bharati exposed Castaneda's well-glossed rip-off of Eastern religious thought in a scholarly collection of essays entitled *The Don Juan Papers*.[20]

As a confirmed Buddhist, *The Empire Strikes Back* director Irvin Kershner admitted, "I wanna introduce some Zen here because I don't want the kids to walk away just feeling that everything is shoot-em-up, but that there's also a little something to think about here in terms of yourself and your surroundings."

The entertainment world has greatly absorbed ideas from the Far East. And the film industry is not the only one capitalizing on the current propagation of Eastern worldviews.

The Beatles were enraptured with the guru of Transcendental Meditation (TM), Maharishi Mahesh Yogi, as well as by A. C. Bhaktivedanta's Hare Krishna movement. In an interview published in the magazine *Update* (December 1983), well-known ex-beatle George Harrison frankly admitted his belief in reincarnation and his reasons for producing songs for and with Hare Krishnas. He confessed that it was a part of his "spiritual service, in order to try to spread the *mantra* all over the world. Also, to try and give the devotees a wider base and a bigger foothold in England and everywhere else." In fact, he claimed that he still gets letters from people saying, " 'I have been in the Krsna temple for three years, and I would have never known about Krsna unless you recorded the *All Things Must Pass* album.' "

Harrison went on to disclose his purpose behind the top-selling record entitled "My Sweet Lord" to which Lord Krishna and other Hindu gods were praised by background singers. He said:

My idea in "My Sweet Lord," because it sounded like a "pop song," was to sneak up on them a bit. The point was to have the people not offended by "Hallelujah"; and by the time it gets to "Hare Krsna," they're already hooked, and their foot's tapping, and they're already singing along "Hallelujah" to kind of lull them into a sense of false security. And then suddenly it turns into "Hare Krsna," and they will be singing that before they know what's happened.[21]

Also heavily influenced by Eastern thought was lead guitarist Mahavishnu John McLaughlin and his jazz-rock group of the seventies called The Mahavishnu Orchestra. On the cover of their album *Birds of Fire* was printed a pantheistic poem by McLaughlin's spiritual mentor, Sri Chimnoy. But the path that pantheism has laid goes deeper and farther than the world of neon-glittered theaters and rock concerts. It has found its way into the spheres of business, science, and education as well.

In the business realm, success scholar Napoleon Hill has stimulated such so-called "success merchants"[22] as Og Mandino, W. Clement Stone, Earl Nightingale, and Norman Vincent Peale. Hill in his best-seller *Think and Grow Rich* proposed that businessmen "draw upon the forces of Infinite Intelligence" because he believed that "the subconscious mind is the connecting link between the finite mind of man and the Infinite Intelligence." In *Your Greatest Power* success motivator J. Martin Kohe further describes this "Mind Power" which is given to every man as "the Infinite Mind Power *of which he is a part*, and through which all desires can come to pass" (emphasis added). Many would be surprised to discover that TM is used by AT&T, General Foods, Connecticut General Life Insurance Co., and Blue Cross/Blue Shield as part of their formal personnel operations.[23] It appears that even the business arena has bought into Eastern pantheism.

Another Eastern-oriented group, Werner Erhard's self-proclaimed "educational corporation" (est), was used by businesses in self-help motivational seminars for their personnel. Est has now been buried by Erhard himself and replaced with what he calls the "Forum." However, besides the cosmetic alterations of his seminar, the basic philosophy remains the same ancient Eastern mysticism that was manifest in est.

Erhard said that "when I get in touch with my self and you get in touch with your self, we will see the same self."[24] And elsewhere, "Self is all there is. I mean that's it."[25] This is clearly the Eastern pantheistic belief that everything is God. Thus, Erhard says that man is the supreme being. Apparently, "Rocky Mountain High" singer and est advisory board member John Denver has taken Erhard up on these claims. For Denver proclaims, "One of these days I'll be so complete I won't be human. I'll be a god."[26]

The world of education has also been affected by Eastern thought. Dr. Beverly Gaylean, former Project Director for three federally funded programs of confluent education in the Los Angeles Public Schools, proposed that

> once we begin to see that we are all God, that we all have the attributes of God, then I think the whole purpose of human life is to reown the Godlikeness within us: the perfect love, the perfect wisdom, the perfect understanding, the perfect intelligence; and when we do that, we create back to that old, that essential oneness which is consciousness.
>
> So my whole view is very much based on that idea. . . . The system of confluent education as I work with it is totally dependent on that view, because my

whole philosophy is that learning is . . . looking within and discovering what information is inside you.[27]

In 1983 Good Apple, Inc. published *Young Scientists Explore Inner and Outer Space: Book 6 Intermediate Level,* by Jerry DeBruin. Its cover includes an illustration of a young boy in a yoga meditation posture with the silhouette of two youngsters looking out at space with a telescope in the background. This particular book includes an unscrambling vocabulary game with words like "meditate," "Zen," "mantra," "mandala," "yoga," "Chakra," and "Buddha," a cutout puzzle of a young boy meditating in front of a Hindu godlike figure, and an imaginary trip into "inner space."

Pantheism has even gripped the science field. In 1973, the Nobel prize winner in physics, Brian Josephson, staked his scientific reputation on the possibility of gaining insights into objective reality by practicing traditional Eastern meditation techniques.

Fritjof Capra wrote *The Tao of Physics: An Exploration of the Parallels Between Modern Physics and Eastern Mysticism* to present his claim that "the two foundations of twentieth-century physics—quantum theory and relativity theory—both force us to see the world very much in the way a Hindu, Buddhist, or Taoist sees it."

Gary Zukav in *The Dancing of the Wu Li Masters: An Overview of the New Physics* tries to demonstrate the parallels between the Hindu picture of Lord Krishna "dancing with all the souls of the world" and modern physics. He says that the "recurrent theme of eastern literature" is that "to dance with god, . . . is to dance with ourselves." He goes on to say that "this is also the direction toward which the new physics, quantum mechanics and relativity, seems to point." The book *Mysticism and the New Physics: A Different Way of Understanding* by Michael Talbot promises to "explore the infinite mysteries of the universe through the age-old wisdom of the East; [and to] explore the occult phenomena which can now be explained."

Such a widespread network of Eastern-oriented groups make up what has been called the "New Age Movement." Marilyn Ferguson, publisher of *Brain/Mind Bulletin,* the most widely read newsletter in the areas of brain research and consciousness, and *The Leading Edge,* a newsletter dealing with the frontiers of social transformation, writes in her book, *The Aquarian Conspiracy:*

> A leaderless but powerful network is working to bring about radical change in the United States. . . . Broader than reform, deeper than revolution, this benign conspiracy for a new human agenda has triggered the most rapid cultural realignment in history. The great shuddering, irrevocable shift overtaking us is . . . a new mind—the ascendance of a startling world view.[28]

In like accord, political activist Mark Satin recognizes that

> a new way of seeing and a new politics is arising *already* in bits and pieces, here and there, across the country. . . . The new politics is arising out of the work and ideas of people in many of the social movements of our time. . . . The new politics is also arising out of the work and ideas of a couple of hundred sympathetic economists and spiritual philosophers, business-people and workers' self-management people, . . . physicists and poets. . . . I have begun to call this politics "New Age politics."[29]

In his book *New Age Politics* Satin lists various New Age organizations such as the Foundation for Inner Peace, Institute for the New Age, Institute for PsychoEnergetics, Institute for the Study of Conscious Evolution, Institute of Noetic Sciences, Meditation Group for the New Age, the Naropa Institute, New Age Feminism, Planetary Citizens, the Zen Center, and a host of others.

Robert Muller, the Assistant Secretary General in charge of coordinating the work of thirty-two specialized agencies and world programs of the United Nations, claims that we are headed for a "new age, a new world . . . a New Genesis, a time global, God-abiding political, moral, and spiritual renaissance to make this planet what it was always meant to be: the Planet of God."[30] Unfortunately, it appears as though Muller's god is the "impersonal force" of Eastern thought, not the heavenly Father of Christianity.

A full-page advertisement for a New Age group called Shinreikyo, entitled "The Fountainhead of Miracles," appeared in *Newsweek* magazine, February 7, 1983. This ad claimed that the "power of Shinreikyo," the "true Shintoism"

> can provide healing, even of cancer and hereditary defects, escape from accidents and calamities, allow painless, natural childbirth, and grant a peaceful transmigration from this life to the next, leaving the body with no signs of death: no rigor mortis, death spots, odor, or lowering of body temperature. . . . It can even influence animals, plants and inanimate objects. . . .
>
> At this moment, our world is undergoing an enormous change comparable to the dawning of the day itself. We are facing the reality of a gigantic Force of Life such as humankind has never experienced before,

which is called, "the coming of the spiritual Sun of the New Age."

The increasing tide of the New Age Movement further demonstrates how our American society is "turning East." This current gravitation toward Eastern thought could provide a reason for our society's current attraction to the Eastern doctrine of reincarnation.

GROWING CONCERN WITH DEATH

I can't say that I think this or do such and such because we all may die tomorrow, but I'm convinced that in all our minds there's an underlying nagging fear that the world could blow up, a fear which today is more silent than in the bomb-shelter era of a few years ago but perhaps even more strongly felt and exhibited in minute, imperceptible ways.[31]

The conclusion of a survey on the attitudes toward death taken in 1971 said that the largest single factor relating to death in the 1970s probably was the threat of atomic bombs. The report also discovered that

readers of *Psychology Today* apparently feel that [death] is more important than sex; the single biggest surprise in the results of the *P.T.* death questionnaire was the sheer volume of response. More than 30,000 readers returned the research questionnaires, and more than 2,000 of them sent substantial letters with their replies. This broke the record set by the *P.T.* sex questionnaire, which fetched somewhat over 20,000 replies. It was almost as though thousands of persons had been waiting for a legitimate occasion to unburden

23

themselves about death and then felt somehow cleansed after writing their unspoken thoughts. Several letters said as much, indicating how grateful the respondents were and how meaningful the exercise had been to them.[32]

Hans Morgenthau, in an essay on "Death in the Nuclear Age," stated that

a secular age, which has lost faith in individual immortality in another world and is aware of the impending doom of the world through which it tries to perpetuate itself here and now, is left without a remedy. Once it has become aware of its condition, it must despair.[33]

On November 20, 1983, ABC Television premiered *The Day After,* a film which fictionally portrayed what would happen as a result of a nuclear confrontation. After the movie, ABC put on a special broadcast called *Viewpoint* where *Nightline* host Ted Koppel led a group of distinctive panelists, including Carl Sagan, William F. Buckley, Henry Kissinger, and Elie Wiesel, in discussing the film and the subject of nuclear war.

Sagan explained how the "overall consequences" of a "major nuclear war" would be "much more dire" than that depicted in the movie. He said that "the biologists who have been studying this thing [i.e., a nuclear disaster] think that there is a real possibility of the extinction of the human species from such a war." At this point, Koppel stopped Sagan from going any further because, he said, "If our viewers were depressed after seeing the movie, I suspect you've brought them to an even greater nadir."

The growing threat of nuclear holocaust has fed man's already innate repulsion toward the grave. And perhaps this concern (maybe even fear) fuels what many theologians would call a natural desire for immortality and therefore, in some circles, reincarnation.

A PSYCHOLOGICAL REMEDY

Another possible reason for the popularity of the belief in reincarnation is the currently popular use of what is called "past-life therapy." This psychological technique assumes the reality of reincarnation, and through hypnosis takes the client back to previous lives in order to aid some present ailment.

Housewife Nita Palmer first went to a past-life recall therapist in 1980 because she felt "kind of blocked up in my everyday life." Extremely busy and feeling pulled in a dozen directions, she felt resentful of the demands being made on her and unable to commit her full energy to anything. Hypnosis brought her back to a lifetime shortly before Christ. She says of the experience,

> I was a man, a member of the Sanhedrin, the leaders of the Jews before the time of Christ. . . . It was horrifying. We were misleading the Jewish people. They were being led to believe that we knew the nature and will of God, and we didn't. In fact, we were working hand in hand with the Roman Government in taxing the people. . . . I was caught in it, did not know how to get out of it. I felt a lot of ambivalence, a lot of self-hatred.[34]

The experience did not go unheeded. As Mrs. Palmer came out of hypnosis, she learned that "if I was willing to withhold something important then, and it bothered me, I could do something about it now, not withhold my energy from my present life." She went on to say that the experience freed up the spiritual blockage she'd been feeling and marked a turning point in her life.

A doctor's receptionist is said to have been unable to stand perfume of any kind. This phobia caused her to personally telephone female patients and ask them not to wear perfume when they had appointments with the doctor. After some of the patients complained to the doctor and she was about to face the unemployment line, she submitted to hypnotic regression.

As an Eskimo woman in a former life, she recalled that she was raped by a man who put his hand over her mouth to keep her quiet during the assault. The stench of whale oil, which is a substance from which ambergris—the base of many modern perfumes—is extracted, exuded from his hands. Past-life recall therapist Dick Sutphen claimed that once she understood why perfume frightened and disgusted her, it never bothered her again.

With more and more people turning to the solutions of psychology for their problems and ailments, there is little wonder that a popular psychological method like past-life therapy is increasing in use. And since this therapy assumes, at least on the part of the client, the reality of reincarnation experiences, perhaps its use as a psychological remedy contributes to the growing popularity of the doctrine itself.

In summary, the reasons for the popularity of reincarnation are many. These include our society's present fascination with Eastern thought, our growing preoccupation with death, and the growing acceptance of the validity of past-life therapy. But what is this strange Eastern belief that has made such an impact? In the next two chapters we will survey various types of reincarnation doctrine.

CHAPTER 2
EAST IS EAST

What is reincarnation? Why is this Eastern belief enjoying such popularity in the Western world today? There is a virtual smorgasbord of reincarnation beliefs of both Eastern and Western varieties. In this chapter, we will concern ourselves with the Eastern types.

DEFINITION AND FORMS
OF REINCARNATION

The word "reincarnation" comes from the Latin *re,* which means "again," and *incarnere,* which comes from two other Latin words, *in* and *caro*—"in flesh." Thus, it literally means "to come again in the flesh." World religions authority Geoffrey Parrinder defines reincarnation as "the belief that the soul or some power passes after death into another body."[1] Sometimes other words, such as transmigration, metempsychosis, palingenesis, and rebirth are used synonymously with the term reincarnation.

Learning new words is sometimes essential in order to finish a crossword puzzle. Likewise, the puzzle of reincarnation has its own vocabulary. It will be necessary for us to learn certain new terms associated with this belief. For when we discuss the idea of reincarnation with a friend or acquaintance who knows about or believes in reincarnation, we need to be familiar with the terms he or she is using. Knowing these terms will also help us to understand material written on reincarnation as well as enable us to discuss it more intelligently.

HINDU VIEWS OF REINCARNATION

Hinduism is the major religion of India, but there are many different Hindu schools of thought. We will concern ourselves with the Vedantic view (that school of Indian thought which bases its philosophy on the writings of the *Upanishads* and the *Vedanta Sutra)* since this theory of reincarnation is in line with that of other orthodox schools of Indian thought.[2]

Indian philosophers Shankara (eighth century) and Ramanuja (eleventh century) taught what are now the two main schools of thought in the Vedantic system. For our purposes, we will label these two different views as the "Impersonal" view (Shankara's *advaita* system) and the "Personal" view (Ramanuja's *vishishtadvaita* system; see Model 1 in Appendix for both views).

Shankara's reincarnation belief is called *advaita,* which means "not-twoness" (everything is one). Shankara's school holds a pantheistic worldview that says God (Brahman) is everything and everything is God. Thus, God is the world and the world is God.[3]

Ramanuja, on the other hand, believed in a distinction between God and the world. His system, called *vishishtadvaita,* meaning "difference no-difference," is not the total opposite of Shankara's system, but is regarded as a modified form of it. In contrast to Shankara, Ramanuja believed that God was personal and that the world and individuals are

God's "body." Thus, he can be regarded as having a "pan-en-theistic" (all-in-God) system where God is more than the world—in a real sense, distinguished from the world—while entailing the world as an aspect of himself as well.[4]

Many basic elements of these reincarnation beliefs dealing with impersonal and Personal views are basically the same. The soul is called the *jiva* or *jivatman*. The soul *(jiva)* is attached to a physical body called the "gross body." At death, this physical body dies and the soul survives as a mental entity called the "subtle body" *(lingua sharira)*.[5]

This subtle body is the continuous element throughout the reincarnation process until salvation occurs. The soul, as the subtle body, bears the karma of its past lives.

Karma literally means "doing, deeds, action, work."[6] Through the process of time, "Karma became both action and its fruit or entail, and was closely linked with the doctrine of transmigration, by which good Karma brought a good afterlife, and evil Karma a bad one."[7] Thus, it is used to mean "you reap what you sow." If we do evil, then evil will be returned to us. If we do good, then good will be returned to us proportionately in the next life.

Hence, the subtle body accumulates its karma of good and/or evil, and based on one's past deeds, karma selects an appropriate rebirth. World religions scholar John B. Noss says,

> One's future existence is determined by the Law of Karma . . . , the law that one's thoughts, words, and deeds have an ethical consequence fixing one's lot in future existences. Looked at retrospectively, karma is the *cause* of what is happening in one's life now.[8]

The subtle body, then, after making the appropriate karmic calculations, attaches itself to a developing embryo.[9]

If in our former life we had "good conduct," then we would enter a "pleasant womb"—be born into a higher socio-religious class. But if our conduct in a past life was not good, then we would enter a "foul and stinking womb"—be born into a lower class as an animal, vegetable, or mineral. Moreover, reincarnation is not limited to this earth. In fact, one can be reborn in a multiplicity of heavens, hells, and purgatories.[10]

The Hindu holds that throughout the continual process of death and rebirth, one slowly progresses toward his salvation, from the bondage of being entrapped in this world to the goal of spiritual perfection in divine self-existence.

However, it is on the nature of this "salvation" that Shankara and Ramanuja disagree. Both have as a goal to break the "wheel" of rebirth. This liberation from the burdensome reincarnation-wheel is called *moksha*.[11]

Shankara's Impersonal view defines *moksha* as "unqualified identity."[12] That is, the self, when it has shed all of its karmic debt, is freed from having to be reincarnated again so that it literally becomes one with God. The *jivatman* (the individual soul) becomes the Brahman (God). Hence, the self loses his/her individuality and merges into God.

On the other hand, the Personal Hindu view of Ramanuja understands *moksha* as retaining the individuality of the soul and of God. "Liberation" is then interpreted as freedom from rebirth so that one may eternally live in a constant devotional relationship with Bhagwan, the personal God.

BUDDHIST VIEWS OF REINCARNATION
Buddhism, the major religion of much of the Far East, is predominantly found in Tibet, China, and Japan. Gautama the Buddha lived in the sixth century B.C. After his death his beliefs spread throughout the world. The fundamental

difference between the Buddhist and the Hindu view of reincarnation is the Buddhist doctrine of "no-self" *(anatta)*. In Hinduism, the self survives bodily death only to be reincarnated again. But according to Buddha there is no self, as·we presently know it, in the "afterlife."[13] In his book *A Sourcebook in Indian Philosophy,* Sarvepalli Radhakrishnan, a famous Hindu statesman and philosopher, says, "There is no such thing in Buddhism as the migration of the soul or the passage of an individual from life to life. . . . It is not the dead man who comes to rebirth but another. There is no soul to migrate."

This difficult doctrine is often illustrated by a wax that is impressed by a seal. The engravings of the seal leave an impression in the wax but no substance is transferred from the seal to the wax. Likewise in rebirth, even though there is a definite characteristic connection between the present life and the future one, nothing substantial is transferred.

The exact nature of this "survival" after death cannot be detailed because it transcends our understanding. The soul, or the soul as we think of it in this life, does not exist.

In our present temporal world, the self is a mind-body unity. At death, all the components of this mind-body unity are dissolved. All that is left is a "karmic deposit of former selves."[14] That which is reincarnated is called *vinnana. Vinnana* is not identical with one's consciousness (which is just one component of one's mind-body unity), but is the unconscious disposition which has "collected" its karmic deposit.

To put it another way, it is the prevailing tendencies of one's character which survive death and re-enter embodiment. After death, the *vinnana* is filled with the craving for material life. This craving "attracts" him back to the physical world and he is thus reborn. (See Model 2 in Appendix.)

As with Hinduism, Buddhism believes that one's karma

determines a person's next life. And yet, Buddha's view of karma was much more flexible than the Hindu version and was regarded as only one of the determining factors in successive rebirths. This is not to dilute the Buddhist belief in the law of karma. It was still regarded as a law and enforcer of equity, matching the right soul with the right body. "Thus karma is often taken to function through the homing of a soul upon a morally and physically appropriate fetus."[15]

Primitive forms of Buddhism affirm the possibility of being reborn as non-human life-forms, while more modern Buddhists consider it an impossibility.[16] Furthermore, rebirths not only take place in different worlds and planes, but in fact, earthly rebirths are regarded as the minority.

The wheel of *samsara* (continual rebirth) is deemed something to be escaped. Through self-discipline, ethical conduct, wisdom, and meditation one can achieve *moksha* (liberation). This state of liberation is called *nirvana.*

What is nirvana? The different schools of Buddhism are divided on precisely what nirvana is. According to Hick, the major views are: (1) minimal Theravada interpretation; (2) orthodox Theravada interpretation; (3) mainline Mahayana interpretation; and (4) Mahayana Amida Buddhism interpretation.

Minimal Theravada interpretation. Nirvana is here understood as merely a psychological state. It only exists in the living Buddhist monk *(arhat)*. This view is in concord with the atheistic belief in final extinction—no afterlife at all.

Orthodox Theravada interpretation. Nirvana is an indescribable reality that goes far beyond our comprehension. It is where the self becomes one with the Infinite transcendent reality.

Mainline Mahayana interpretation. While some believe nirvana means extinction, Buddha taught that nirvana could be attained in this life because he himself had experienced it. The annihilation spoken of in the state of nirvana more probably refers to the annihilation of desires, for to be rid of cravings is to escape the burdensome wheel of rebirth.

A further distinction between the Mahayanist and Theravadin interpretation of nirvana is that whereas the latter separates *samsara* (the wheel of rebirth) from nirvana (liberation from the wheel), the Mahayanist meshes them together. Liberation is attained when one realizes that *samsara is* nirvana.

Mahayana Amida Buddhism interpretation. When the unfaithful in "loving trust" call upon the Buddha, he confers his merit freely on them so that they are reborn in the Pure Land. This is the place of paradise where it is very possible to attain nirvana. However, "gradually paradise, rather than nirvana, came to be the key hope in the religious imagination of Pure Land Buddhists."[17]

JAINISM

Jainas, followers of an ancient (ninth century B.C.) religion of India, believe that there is a permanent soul or self *(jiva)* which persists throughout its afterlife. Throughout one's reincarnations, one accumulates various kinds of karma-like "layers" or "incrustations" which cover and weigh down the soul. These layers must be worn off through the process of reincarnation or by self-discipline, asceticism, and perfect knowledge *(kevala)*.[18]

Under the Jain system, one can be reborn in non-human forms at various levels of existence. The accumulation of karmic matter is in direct proportion to one's desires. The worse the desires, the heavier the form of karmic matter which is embedded on the soul, sinking the soul to a lower scale of existence. If one is to reach a higher level of existence, he must shed his heavy karmic matter and rise up to the lighter existence of the "eternal home." There, the worthy soul is not reduced to nothingness but retains its own individual consciousness. (See Model 3 in Appendix.)

SIKHISM

Like Jainism, Sikhs believe that to succumb to material desires is to accumulate karma. But unlike Jainism, their reincarnation system holds that the ultimate end of the dedicated Sikh is absorption into God. (See Model 3.)

> Let them think only of God, endlessly repeat his name, and be absorbed into Him; in such absorption alone lies the bliss known to Hindus as Nirvana. For salvation is not going to Paradise after a last judgment, but absorption—in God, the True Name.[19]

ISKCON

According to A. C. Bhaktivedanta Swami Prabhupada, the founder of the International Society of Krishna Consciousness (ISKCON or Hare Krishnas), the Hindu Scriptures called the *Vedas* teach that there are 8,400,000 species of life, from amoebas to humans and "demigods."[20] Our whole existence in the material world is a result of our karma from past experiences.

The determination of one's future rebirth is a dual effort by oneself and Lord Krishna. A person determines his own desires and Lord Krishna supplies the "material energy" needed to fulfill those desires. The more one gives in to his sensual and material desires, the lower the life-form in which he will be reincarnated. However, if he sheds these "lowly" desires, then he will progress to higher forms of existence until he is liberated from the process of reincarnation altogether.

It is only through a human body that our souls can attain liberation. Unfortunately, a human reincarnation is a rarity and only occurs "after evolving through millions of lower species." Thus, Prabhupada says, "One who misuses the human form and does not become self-realized is no better than a dog or an ass."[21]

The way to rid oneself of karma is through chanting a mantra. But in order to be effective the Hare Krishna mantra must be received from a bona fide master in the spiritual line of disciples descending from Lord Krishna himself. It is only by the mercy of such a qualified *guru* that one can become free from the cycle of birth and death.

"Back to Godhead" is the theme of ISKCON liberation since liberation is seen as a literal "homecoming" from where one originally fell. All living beings originally existed "in the spiritual world as transcendental loving servants of God."[22] The unnatural cycle of repeated birth, disease, old age, and death can be stopped when one's consciousness is dovetailed with the supreme consciousness of God. Furthermore, this ultimate end of liberation is guaranteed for all. The soul is never banished to eternal damnation.

SUMMARY

Although there are many forms of Eastern reincarnation, most of them have several things in common. Keeping these similarities in mind may prove helpful in understanding Eastern reincarnation as a whole.

Goal of perfection. Reincarnation advocates assume a goal of perfected humanity. This can be summarily described as a moral, spiritual, and in some instances, "bodily" perfection.

Gradual evolutionary progression. They would agree that perfection cannot (or at least, most likely will not) be attained instantaneously. Perfection comes about through a slow, gradual process.

Doctrine of "second chance." While not all of them affirm universalism where all are guaranteed final salvation, they all agree that one lifetime is not enough to reach perfection. Hence, an abhorrence to the traditional doctrine of hell and the acceptance of a doctrine of "second chance."

Doctrine of karma. Karma is a general characteristic of Eastern pantheism. What one sows in this life, he reaps in the next life. Past lives influence or determine future ones.

Survival of the self. With the exception of Buddhism, they all assert the survival, in some form or another, of the self in successive afterlives. The self persists throughout its rounds in the continual wheel of rebirth.

Multiple perishable bodies. Whatever the nature of the body suggested by the different proponents, the reincarnated body is always perishable so that the self can be reincarnated again.

Multiple worlds or realms. Most agree that reincarnations do not have to take place exclusively on planet Earth. They could take place on other planets, in other solar systems, universes, dimensions.

CHAPTER 3
WEST IS EAST

(SEE ALSO p.7)

Although reincarnation is often thought to be an Eastern belief, it has deep roots in the ancient Western world as well. These roots began in ancient Greece and continued through Roman and medieval times into the modern world. Today some 20–25 percent of Europeans believe in some form of reincarnation.[1] Belief in reincarnation is not unique to the East. The West has had its share of reincarnation beliefs which we will survey in the following sections.

ANCIENT GREEK AND ROMAN VIEWS OF REINCARNATION

PYTHAGORAS

The sixth century B.C. philosopher Pythagoras is believed to have held to the doctrine of the transmigration of the soul to another life. While we have no direct record of Pythagoras's position on reincarnation, two other Greek philosophers attest to Pythagoras's belief in this ancient doctrine of rebirth. Empedocles, who probably was reiterating the teaching of Pythagoras, claimed that the cause of transmigration of the soul was sin and that it lasted 30,000 years until one eventually became a god. The early Pythago-rean philosopher Pindar held that only the evil were con-demned to transmigration.

PLATO

One of the most prominent Greek philosophers of the an-cient world was Plato (fourth century B.C.). In his books *Gorgias, Meno, Phaedo,* and the *Republic,* the idea of mul-tiple rebirths is evident. According to Plato, man is

> a soul in a body, and his soul needs to grow toward the highest good, that it may no longer have to suffer continued rebirth but go into that state in which it may, like God, behold and enjoy forever the hierarchy of the ideal forms, in all their truth, beauty, and good-ness.[2]

Plato taught that "we ought to try to escape from the earth to the dwelling of the gods as quickly as we can; and to escape is to become like God, so far as [that] is possible."

PLOTINUS

Perhaps the most developed system of reincarnation in this age came from the Neo-Platonic philosopher Plotinus of the third century A.D.[3] Plotinus claimed that there were basically three spheres of existence: the vegetative, the sen-sitive, and the intellective. The vegetative sphere is, of course, the realm of non-sensual, non-intelligent plant life. The sensitive sphere is basically the world of animals. Men and gods dwell in the place of the intellective. (See Model 1 in Appendix.)

Even though Plotinus did not speak of karma, he did have the concept of past actions determining future reincar-nations. He said that "when the life-principle leaves the body it is what it is, what it most intensely lived." If one is "lethargic," then he will be reborn as a plant. Those who continually seek their own sensual gratification will

> become animals—corresponding in species to the particular temper of the life—ferocious animals where the sensuality has been accompanied by a certain measure of spirit, gluttonous and lascivious animals where all has been appetite and satiation of appetite.[4]

Moreover, reincarnation may serve as a punishment as well. "Cruel masters become slaves; those who have misused their wealth become paupers. The murderer is murdered himself; the ravisher is reborn as a woman and suffers the same fate."[5] Like many of the reincarnation models we have studied thus far, Plotinus also believed that reincarnated souls could inhabit other planets.

The souls which liberated themselves from sensual desires and therefore from the cycle of reincarnation will dwell "where there is reality and true being and the divine, in God." Hence, according to Plotinus, the goal for man is to become one with God.

AN AFRICAN VIEW OF REINCARNATION

While some scholars hold that in tropical Africa the belief in reincarnation is deeply enrooted, others, like Innocent C. Onyewuenyi, argue that

> what the Africans mean by "return" or "reborn" cannot be translated by "reincarnation" because for them the child or children are not *identical* with the dead, since the birth of the little one(s) in no wise puts an end to the existence of the deceased ancestor in the spirit-world.[6]

In light of the elements of the African conception of the afterlife, Onyewuenyi's analysis certainly seems justified.

According to this African perspective, a person dies, enters the spirit world, and his vital force returns to earth in his descendents. There is no concept of the progress of the soul as it returns to the material world. Nor is there a sense of punishment where evil men return in lower life-forms. However, they do believe that some tribes are related to certain animals and therefore can return as animals.

Yet this process of returning to earth should not be regarded as reincarnation. The deceased "self" is not re-embodied. For one retains his own identity in the spirit world even though he can influence or determine the physical and psychological characteristics of a newborn in his family. It is difficult to understand the logic of a belief in an ancestor who in some sense "returns" to this world and yet does not leave the other world. Yet this is the inconsistent view held by many tropical Africans.

THEOSOPHY: A EUROPEAN/AMERICAN VIEW OF REINCARNATION

Many of the publications that promote the doctrine of reincarnation are published by the Theosophical Publishing House or the Theosophical University Press. The Theosophical Society claims to be a unifier and peacemaker in religion. This modern form of Hindu and Buddhist philosophy intends to accomplish its global vision by merging the East with the West. Its leaders, Helena Blavatsky, Annie Besant, and Alice Bailey are also credited with being some of the foremost visionary leaders of the New Age Movement.

Theosophy teaches that since we are souls which emanated from God, we once "possessed all the powers of our divine Father." Thus the purpose of reincarnation is "to bring to us these experiences which will most rapidly awaken all our latent faculties and bring them into action."[7]

Souls retain their sexless personhood throughout the reincarnation process, returning to earth as an embryo. The nature of this "return" is determined by karma, a manifestation of the universal law of cause and effect. In this way, "the law of karma motivates rebirth. Reincarnation is made necessary by the accumulation of good and evil actions brought forward from previous existences. Rebirth must continue as long as karma remains.[8] However, theosophists reject the notion that a human soul could be reincarnated into non-human forms.

After death, the soul enters an intermediate state called *Kamaloka,* the "auric sphere," or the "astral world" which is identical to that of the "subtle body" of Hinduism. Here in this purgatorial state, individuals suffer for past sins in order to "work off impurities."

The state of purgatory or the reincarnation in this world of suffering may constitute "temporary hells" and "temporary heavens," but there are no permanent, "static" ones. The escape from the "cycle of necessity" is the ultimate destiny of all. Instead of heaven, G. de Purucker looks toward an

> endless progress, endless advancement for all, excluding none, the tiniest atom, the mightiest god, two different stages of growing entities. The atom becomes a man, the man becomes a god, the god becomes a super-god, and so on *ad infinitum*.[9]

He boldly proclaims,

> I want to grow out of a man to be a god, to lose my manhood, to merge into godhood; and when I become

a god, I shall still have, I hope, this yearning, this unsatisfied hunger for something grander and greater still than godhood, always marching upwards and on- wards.[10]

The nature of the final state, according to their perspec- tive, is difficult to determine. Bailey calls it a "stage of Christlike perfection."[11] De Purucker says that this is when the soul "comes into direct and intimate relation, spiritual relation, communion, self-identification, with the Divine mind of which it is a child, the spark, the offspring. Then you have Reality. That is Nirvana."[12] And yet this is not a total identification and absorption into "God." For de Purucker rejects the assertion that we are swallowed up into a state which dissolves our individual consciousness. (See Model 4 in Appendix.)

SO-CALLED "CHRISTIAN" VIEWS OF REINCARNATION

EDGAR CAYCE

Cayce was a Sunday school teacher who, at the turn of the twentieth century, made near perfect diagnoses in technical medical terms while in a trance. This is even more astound- ing when one realizes that Cayce only had a sixth-grade education. After about two decades of making these amaz- ing medical diagnoses in his "sleep-state," Cayce began to give readings on theology and philosophy. These readings included affirmations of the doctrine of reincarnation.

The voice which spoke to and through Cayce claimed that originally God had projected out of his Being other beings which took on animal forms. These beings became entrapped within their bodies and so God created human bodies in order to help them escape![13] Once in human form, these souls could then proceed to work off their accumulated karma. And so Cayce, like the ancients of the East, taught that "the sole purpose of reincarnation of the individual soul is to destroy the accumulated karma."[14]

According to Cayce, even Jesus had karma that needed to be worked off. The difference between Christ and us is that he perfectly shed his karma, while we have not. Thus, Christ is "the way-shower." He modeled the way to God for us by his atonement ("at-one-ment"). "He is thy karma if you will but accept him."[15] The "law of grace" is that Christ has given us the opportunity to atone for our own sins. When one sheds the shackles of karma, he is free to enter into eternal life. Only then can he return to his original inheritance as a portion of God himself.

The readings of Cayce emphasize God-realization as the true purpose of reincarnation. Cayce advocates, like many other reincarnation models we have already surveyed, the doctrine of universalism which claims that no soul was ever created to perish and all will eventually be saved.[16] The only God the sleeping Edgar Cayce knew was a loving God of infinite mercy, who has already forgiven us all. (See Model 4 in Appendix.)

QUINCY HOWE, JR.

Quincy Howe, Jr., is an associate professor of classics at Scripps College and a graduate of Harvard, Columbia, and Princeton. Howe said that "the reincarnationist would describe the cosmos, not as a creation, but as an emanation from God."[17] Hence, each person is, in essence, divine.

However, for some unexplained reason man, in a state of God-consciousness, "forgot" his divine origin and nature. This, for the reincarnationist, was the fall of man. And so, man's fundamental purpose in life is to move toward full, conscious realization of his own divinity. This movement is accomplished through the process of reincarnation. After death and before reincarnation takes place,

> ... the length of repose between lives is in direct proportion to the virtue and spirituality of one's incarnate life. ... Thus the intervals are seen as quiescent periods during which the soul recovers from its sorrows and mistakes and reaps the benefit of its good acts.[18]

During this time, it is supposed that the Eastern doctrine of karma begins to help shape the destiny of the incarnation to come. No action escapes the notice of karmic law. Every situation in which a man finds himself can finally be traced back to his karma.

And yet, we should note that while the retribution of karma is certain, it is not necessarily immediate. In other words, the effect of a present action might *not* take place in the next life. It may not even manifest itself for many lifetimes to come. For "the fruit of the act does not come until the individual is fully ready to receive it."[19]

Karma must be admitted without impugning God's love and justice. In fact, God is the one who both ordains the law of karma and helps man to emerge triumphant at last from his hardships.

Howe prefers to understand the ancient Eastern view of animal incarnations as allegorical and warns man not to sink into bestial conduct. A literal approach to animal incarnations would defeat the whole purpose of humanity's spiritual progress in the course of reincarnation. However, Howe does leave room in his system, in only extreme cases, for human beings to lose all claim to human incarnation.

Nevertheless, as a general rule, a person progresses in an evolutionary way to his final goal through many human incarnations. For the reincarnationist, evolution is a key concept to accept and understand:

> In fact, to embrace the doctrine of reincarnation is to accept the necessity of evolution. Reincarnation makes sense both ethically and theologically in that it demands and ensures the evolution of all.[20]

Just as evolution in the natural realm is universal, so also is evolution in the spiritual realm universal. All will go through the process of reincarnation, and thus, all have the implicit guarantee of final success.

The "Christian" progresses to the point of God-realization when at the very end of reincarnation he finally experiences the fullness of divine union. This is when "the soul at last knows beyond all doubt that God is its essence and inheritance." At last, the soul will remember "the full and perfect identity between this Atman [the individual human soul] and Brahman who is God as the unmanifest Absolute."[21]

One can see in this last model of harmonization that Howe has propagated, as Hugo Culpepper claims, "essentially pure Hinduism."[22] There is very little difference fundamentally between the Hindu conception of reincarnation and Howe's so-called "Christian" version of it. (See Model 4 in Appendix.)

FREDERICK SPENCER

Frederick Spencer is another writer who wishes to reconcile reincarnation with Christianity. Spencer rejects the transmigration of souls from human into animal bodies. He does, however, hold to the long length of time (at least, longer than a lifetime) that it takes to reach perfection. He affirms that this perpetuation of reincarnational progression will not last forever. There will be an end to continual dying. And while he rebuts any extreme form of the doctrine of karma, he nevertheless recognizes that, with the aid of what he calls "judgment, . . . moral variations unfit for the Kingdom of God are eliminated."[23]

Spencer includes universalism in his system. In fact, "the salvation of the most sinfully obstinate can only be a matter of time, provided, that is, the least vestige of rational freedom and moral sensibility remain." For "the liberty of independence is mighty, but the love of God is mightier."[24]

Along with universalism, Spencer seems to believe in the pantheistic absorption conception of the final relationship between humanity and God. The state of perfection is where we are "reabsorbed" until absolute union will result. (See Model 4 in Appendix.)

RUDOLF FRIELING

The German scholar Rudolf Frieling proposes a reincarnation model which combines Christianity with Rudolf Steiner's Anthroposophy. Steiner was a Theosophist who developed a philosophy which became known as Anthroposophy ("the wisdom of man"). According to his model, man is believed to be on his way in a spiritual evolution to Christ-consciousness. In addition, the soul or ego analyzes and decides what his next life will be like, according to the heredity traits available to him and his own "etheric and soul forces." The ego can also control the good and bad causes and consequences from previous incarnations.

This stage in the spirit world after death is one of relative bliss and progression. Its limits are determined by the previous life. Three stages of progression are arranged according to one's development and its correspondent "supersensible powers."[25]

This process of moving through the various stages after death involves the discarding of unacceptable elements in the human soul so that "the spiritual core of man" journeys to even higher regions of the spirit-world. His next earthly incarnation is then planned with the angelic world and "akin" human souls.

Steiner claims that "centuries lie between separate incarnations, though there are exceptions." Moreover, the process of reincarnation is not endless. After many intermediate judgments, there follows a "Last Judgment." This Last Judgment will result

> in a division of mankind between those who have made good use of their lives on earth and those who have slighted the chances offered them. Lastly it will be decisive whether Christ has been received by man or not. Without accepting what has entered into the evolution of mankind through Christ, man cannot fulfill his task of becoming Man.[26]

Then, man is met by Christ as Christ lowers himself through the multileveled regions to the lowest level of the "supersensible realm," known as the " 'etheric' realm of lifegiving and formative forces." Just as at this time man becomes aware of this realm and meets Christ "face to face," so also in some remote future, as the supersensible faculties of man increase, he will meet Christ at an even higher level—the "spiritual realm." Ultimately, on a higher level still, there will be "a meeting of the true human ego, then fully awakened, with the Ego of Christ." In line with this progression, "reincarnation becomes increasingly obvious since thereby men pass through the great evolutionary phases and are allowed to share ever more conscious and intimate meetings with Christ."[27] (See Model 5 in Appendix.)

GEDDES MACGREGOR

Geddes MacGregor is Distinguished Professor Emeritus of Philosophy at the University of Southern California and an Anglican priest. MacGregor believes that reincarnation is "an enrichment of the Christian hope."[28] And as such, "reincarnation, whatever else it may be, *means* resurrection of some kind. The attainment of a 'glorified' body might be through a gradual process."[29]

MacGregor believes that reincarnation should be seen in the light of evolution since they are parallel. Whereas evolution entails the idea of the struggle for biological development, reincarnation can be seen as "a counterpart in the struggle for moral development." An instantaneous perfection is repugnant to MacGregor. "Salvation, however quickly assured (as some Christians believe to be), is not quickly achieved." In fact, he believes that we should "expect a long evolutionary, purgatorial process. The task is not only too complex and too arduous to be quickly accomplished; it is of such a nature that setbacks are to be expected."[30]

Purity cannot be achieved rapidly; MacGregor believes that it comes through a long, evolutionary process of moral growth. And once we accept the notion of an intermediate or purgatorial state, "a form of reincarnation would fit the case perfectly." Thus, the ancient doctrine of *samsara*—the wheel of rebirth—he sees as a series of "purgatorial steps." While most Catholics believe in an "other-worldly" purgatory, MacGregor proposes a "this-worldly" purgatory. What controls this purgatorial process is karma: "Karma, . . . is inseparable from the spiritual side of the evolutionary coin. It is the principle of evolution understood in specifically moral terms."[31]

Such a doctrine, he believes, protects us from fostering

the apparent "arbitrariness" of the notion of "divine judgment." Karma is automatic. But it does not negate "the notion of mercy and forgiveness." In this way, God can be pictured as "finding ways of overcoming the moral law of karma, as he is seen by some to find ways of overcoming nature."[32]

Moreover, God's compassion allows us an unlimited amount of time to work out our salvation, since karma leads us on the most direct path to higher consciousness and eternal life. Also, karma is just because we are the ones who create it:

> We create our own karma by our own acts. Karma is the given . . . and our task is to extricate ourselves from it . . . by surmounting it and so creating new and hopefully better karma. I have created the prison from which I must now extricate myself.[33]

To think that the human soul can transmigrate to the body of a beast, however, is a "cruder, unethical form" of reincarnation. Reincarnations involving punishment in purgatory are limited to humans.

MacGregor rejects "the standard Christian alternative" to reincarnation, namely, the "horrible" doctrine of hell, because it contradicts the "fundamental Christian assertion that God is love." MacGregor recognizes the fact that even after thousands of lifetimes, whether in this galaxy or another, there may still be those who fail to grow in any direction at all. And he concedes that nothing could be served by the continuation of the futile process. This, however, does not lead MacGregor to accept the existence of a conscious hell. Instead, he interprets hell as "final extinction."[34]

MacGregor holds that for those who do progress and go to heaven there is no absorption into God or any sort of deification. They will gain a new kind of body as they move into the ultimate state where they will behold God.

But this will not be the final state of embodiment, and thus, growth. The whole world will go through an evolutionary change which "will be the end of man *as he now is* and the consummation of *his* world." And yet, man will have to achieve this transformation himself. MacGregor assures us, however, that "the Christian good news" is still intact. For "while without the redeeming work of Christ we could not hope to accomplish that self-transformation of humanity, with Christ we can and we shall."[35]

MacGregor's model can be summarized as one which attempts to see each reincarnation as a resurrection. He believes that reincarnation enables one to receive a new capacity to be more intimate with God. And perhaps, at the end of every age, an evolutionary "leap" toward perfection will be in store for all humanity. (See Model 6 in the Appendix.)

MICHAEL PERRY

Even though Archdeacon of Durham Michael Perry does not favor the belief in reincarnation, he entertains two theories which he believes would enable the Christian to accept reincarnation. His first theory (see Model 7) proposes that human beings consist of "parts" which disengage at death in order to follow their own reincarnated destinies. It is assumed that once the individual parts have reached the final step to perfection they become whole again. Perry has even suggested that

> perhaps different segments have to incarnate one by one until the whole has been exposed to the test of

life on this earth, and can then move on as a totality
to fresh pilgrimages in an extra-terrestrial environment."[36]

In other words, each part or segment of the self progresses
unequally and, therefore, as each segment attains perfection, they are closer to a time when they will be recomposed.

Perry's second theory (see Model 8) is a many-optioned
approach to the afterlife. He asks, "Why should the options
be limited to the simple three of extinction for all, survival
for all, and reincarnation for all?" After all,

> is God not capable of tailoring our future to the needs
> of our present and the constraints that our past have
> put upon the personality which now describes us?
> Perhaps reincarnation is only necessary for some and
> not for all?[37]

Some of us may be reincarnated and others will not. God
will supervise the process and decree what will be best for
the individual. Perhaps those who met Christ in this life
will go directly to the heavenlies, while those who did not
will go in the next life or the one after that. In this way,
reincarnation "would be like returning to re-sit an examination in which we have not done well enough to proceed to
another level of our education."[38]

Perry feels more "theologically" comfortable with "a
scheme which involves a series of lives in a series of future
worlds than of one which requires us to come back here
time and time again." One of the reasons for this is because
if we were to keep coming back to this particular world,
"reincarnation would be a punishment, not a promise."
Furthermore, Perry is a universalist. He says, "All of

us . . . are destined to be resurrected, when God has had his will with us and we have accepted his gift."[39]

JOHN J. HEARNEY

Another scholar, John J. Hearney, who teaches theology at Fordham University, asks, "Why should this law of slow maturing in the evolutionary process operate everywhere in the universe but end suddenly with a person's death?"[40] He speculates that reincarnation is a rare event reserved for a few.

Hearney's harmonization attempt to incorporate reincarnation into Christianity is qualified with a warning: Do not affirm "a doctrine of karma bereft of grace" because to do this would make reincarnation "totally incompatible with the God of Christianity." Thus in Hearney's reincarnation model a person still makes his way to God through the grace of Christ. (See Model 8 in Appendix.)

WILLIAM L. DE ARTEAGA

De Arteaga believes that reincarnation should only be seen as an option for some, but not as necessary for all. At death, the Lord, not karma, directs the destiny of the individual soul "along the path best suited for its development."[41]

The afterlife is multileveled: Those who are not reincarnated go to "quasi-heaven" (i.e., the "bosom of Abraham"), one of the various levels of heaven, or to one of the sheol-hades states. The unbeliever goes to one of the sheol-hades states (which he does not identify with ultimate hell) and then is reincarnated into a state which provides him with an occasion to "choose to enter the kingdom of God."

On the other hand, believers can either enter one of the levels of heaven or reincarnate to a higher level of effective service to the body of Christ. (De Arteaga's view constitutes one of the major differences between a so-called "Christian" conception of reincarnation and an Eastern one.)

Furthermore, de Arteaga believes that the "Christian" conception entails a final Last Judgment. There will come a time when one will have to make a final decision and thus enter either the kingdom of God or ultimate hell. Recalling Scripture, de Arteaga notes there is no forgiveness for those who reject Christ (Heb. 6:1-6). Thus, he believes "a Christian understanding would not be shackled by Eastern assumptions."[42] (See Model 9 in Appendix.)

JOHN H. HICK

Danforth Professor of Philosophy of Religion John H. Hick makes a distinction between "eschatologies" (" 'pictures' of the ultimate state") and "pareschatologies" (" 'pictures' of what happens between death and that ultimate state").

While eschatology is the doctrine of "last things," pareschatology is the doctrine of "next-to-last things." The former involves one's ultimate state, whereas the latter is concerned with that period of the human condition between one's present life and ultimate state. Thus, we have three general areas or levels of a person's life: the life at present, the intermediate state (the pareschaton), and the future life (the eschaton).

Unlike the other "Christian" models of reincarnation, Hick does not advocate the doctrine of "past lives" reincarnationism. For while he does not find such a belief to be theologically objectionable, he finds the logical difficulties connected with the concept of personal identity too serious to ignore. What Hick does propose is a doctrine of many successive lives in many worlds with the individual ultimately reaching a state of human unity which is like the trinitarian conception of God.[43]

Hick proposes a "replica theory" wherein the resurrection of the person can be thought of as a divine re-creation in another place of an exact replica of the deceased person. He argues that it is logically possible for any number of separate worlds to exist which are all observed by God's universal consciousness. "When an individual dies in our present world in space number one he is either immediately or after a lapse of time re-created in a world in space number two."[44] This replica is identical to the deceased in physical appearance as well as in the memory of his former life. Hence, he regards himself as being the same person as the now dead person. "So personal continuity and identity is ensured, even though there is no literal physical continuity between the earthly person and the 'replica.' "[45]

This replica theory now enables Hick to propose a reincarnation model which involves the "resurrection" of an individual in different worlds. According to Hick, a person's present life on planet Earth is his *first* life. The series of reincarnations begins after this earthly life ends.

As for the state between death and rebirth, Hick utilizes the idea of the *bardo* state, which is taken from the *Bardo Thodol* or the *Tibetan Book of the Dead.* This *"bardo* experience is a projection of the individual's own imagination, so that its form depends upon that person's operative beliefs and expectations." Thus, a Buddhist will envision his *bardo* state according to the effects his religion has made on him. Likewise, the Christian will see his intermediate state, most probably, as he thought it would be. A person would "create his or her *bardo* world out of his memory of earth, so that such a next world would be very much like the present world."[46] Hick does not speculate any further in regard to the new worlds.

After a particular length of time in the *bardo* state, "according to the needs of the individual, there is another period of embodiment, which Christians anticipate as the resurrection."[47] Another novel distinction Hick makes in contrast to most reincarnation conceptions is the proposal that the present this-world-self will be translated or resurrected in her new world *without* digressing back to an infant. In other words, while the individual will be reincarnated, she will not be re*born*. Furthermore, he thinks that one will continue to be a sexual being.

We have basically traced the process of Hick's pareschatology. After one has died in the new world, he will presumably enter into another *bardo* experience which will give way to another incarnation/resurrection in another new world. The number of worlds are, of course, unknown (though finite); it will depend upon one's progress as he strives "to reach the point at which he transcends ego-hood and attains the ultimate unitive state, or nirvana."[48]

The need for such an evolutionary process toward the final goal comes with the rejection of instantaneous perfection at the moment of death. For in order to achieve "perfected humanity," human beings must exercise "their freedom in response to the challenges and opportunities of history."[49] Therefore, "there must ... be further time beyond death in which the process of perfecting can continue."[50]

Hick seems to propose that the ultimate state is a harmonious relationship between all perfected and resurrected human beings as well as with God. In short, he attempts to harmonize reincarnation with Christianity by demonstrating the "compatibility" between the resurrection and its Eastern counterpart. While Hick himself admits that he adheres essentially to the Hindu or Buddhist view of reincarnation, it is difficult to understand why he claims that his postulation of reincarnations taking place on many worlds diverges significantly from the Eastern views, for many of these assert the same beliefs. (See Model 10 in the Appendix.)

SUMMARY

As we have seen, the Eastern views on reincarnation have had a long history in the West. Western views, however, have their own characteristic features.

First, Western forms of reincarnation are generally less strictly pantheistic (the belief that all is God), opting for some kind of eventual individual survival, or at least opposed to ultimate absorption into God.

Second, due to Christian influence, many Western forms of reincarnation offer some kind of forgiveness foreign to native Eastern views, thus breaking the rigid law of karma.

Third, many Western views on reincarnation see it as only one of several possible futures for individuals rather than as the destiny for all.

Despite these differences, Eastern and Western types of reincarnation share many common features. They affirm the following:

1. A goal of ultimate perfection for the human race.
2. An evolutionary progress toward perfection which one achieves through reincarnations.
3. In some sense the conduct of one's past lives will influence the kind of lives he will supposedly have in future incarnations.
4. The doctrine of "second chance" after this life.
5. Survival of the self in successive afterlives.
6. The perishability of the bodies into which the reincarnations occur.
7. The existence of multiple worlds or realms in which the reincarnations take place.

CHAPTER 4
PSYCHOLOGY AND REINCARNATION

"Who *was* I?" While the sixties and seventies were years marked with the search for one's identity in the here and now, the search in the eighties seems to be a quest for one's identity in the past. And so the question today is not so much "Who *am* I?" but "Who *was* I?"

Recently many reincarnationists have claimed that the findings of modern psychology support the reality of reincarnation. One of their arguments is that it works. Many patients who "remember" previous lives during past-life therapy get cured of their phobias, disorders, and other psychological problems. Also, facts are revealed by the person who remembers her past life that could not be known unless she actually had been that person of the past.

Let's take a closer look at each of these "evidences" that some say are suggestive of reincarnation.

IF IT WORKS, IS IT RIGHT?

The advocates of reincarnation argue that since past-life recall, whether true or not, brings about the desired results, it must be all right.

Past-life therapy involves the patient undergoing hypnosis in order to journey back and recall a previous life. The theory operating here is that some psychological problems are rooted in the problems of a former self. So, for example, a patient can learn to get over his phobia about swimming once he discovers that he drowned in a previous life.

Parapsychologist Ian Stevenson, perhaps the most respected investigator of past-life recalls, enthusiastically told his colleagues,

> The idea of reincarnation may contribute to an improved understanding of such diverse matters as: phobias and philias of childhood; skills not learned in early life; abnormalities of child-parent relationships; vendettas and bellicose nationalism; childhood sexuality and gender identity confusion; birthmarks, congenital deformities, and internal diseases; differences between members of monozygotic twin pairs; and abnormal appetites during pregnancy.[1]

Even though Dallas psychic Maxine Stantion admits that past-life recall is "all creative imagination," she uses past-life regression when her clients ask for it because of its effectiveness. She says, "It answers a lot of questions. It gives people a whole new perspective. . . . It gives people hope, and I'm for hope."[2]

Notice that whether reincarnation is true or not is irrelevant to this argument in support of past-life therapy. Steff Samuson, a hypnotherapist with the Center for Creative Change, says, "It doesn't matter if it's real or imagined if it helps someone [sic] make sense out of their lives. . . . If it works, who cares?"[3]

In a telephone interview from his Malibu, California,

headquarters, Dick Sutphen told *Dallas Times Herald* reporter Jennifer Boeth that "very often, a person will tap into the cause of a problem in his present life, and just knowing that will immediately relieve the problem. . . . Wisdom erases karma." Moreover,

> even Sutphen, the high priest of past-lives exploration, admits that he's not sure exactly what it is his trainees are experiencing. "If there's a positive result, I don't care what it is," he said, "because it's served the individual well."[4]

William de Arteaga is not totally pragmatic in his approach, though good results play a large part in his acceptance of past-life recall. De Arteaga finds past-life visions (PLVs) useful in his ministry of inner healing but takes the client no deeper than a trance level where the subject still has his will and values. He insists that the client repeatedly say "Jesus is Lord" to assure that he is protected from demonic influence. In short, it is acceptable "Christian" counseling if it works.[5]

The pragmatic justification for using the concept of reincarnation in counseling regardless of its reality raises many problems, the first of which is the foundational belief that what works is acceptable practice. For example, we could lie about our child's age so that he could see a movie at a cheaper price—but would that make it true? Or, we could probably get away with cheating on our income tax—but does this change the fact of how much we made?

Second, hypnosis has recently been found to be a very unreliable source for truth (see the next section for further discussion). If hypnotism is unreliable, how can we trust its results when it is used for past-life recall? Dallas analyst

Dr. James Hall has found that data culled from the imagination is virtually indistinguishable from past-life data. He told the *Dallas Times Herald* that past-life recollections are "the same kind of material you get from dreams."

Third, Dr. Hall thinks that the reliance on past-life recall for a cure can actually be a hindrance to a permanent solution to one's problems. People might "use what they believe to be a past-life experience as an excuse to avoid dealing with things in their present lives." One needs to face his problems rather than retreat to the comfort of blaming a past life.

Fourth, studies have demonstrated that immediate positive results from hypnotism only constitute a temporary victory over a person's problems. Relapses often follow. The pain which was "cured" may return, and sleep may turn again into sleeplessness.

Even worse than the probability of only a temporary cure is the prospect of what is called "symptom substitution." An example of symptom substitution might be a person who developed ulcers after having been relieved of migraine headaches through hypnosis. The Diamond Headache Clinic in Chicago conducted a study which discovered that of "those migraine patients who had learned to control headaches through biofeedback [which relies on the same principles as hypnotherapy], two-thirds reported the development of new psychosomatic symptoms within five years."[6]

Past-life therapy may lead to disastrous results—the "cure" ending up worse than the "disease." And even if it did solve the psychological disorder, what works is not always right. Deceiving clients into thinking that they have actually lived in a previous life is no more ethical than for a doctor to tell a distraught woman that her husband is doing well when he knows that death is imminent.

DO PAST-LIVES FACTS PROVE PAST LIVES?

When Grandpa reminisces about "the good old days," we assume that he knows what he is talking about because he was actually there. In the same way, many reincarnationists argue that the knowledge of facts from the past which a person could not have known demonstrates familiarity with that time period. Such factual familiarity has often been verified.

For example, patients under hypnosis, without any prior knowledge of a foreign language, have been able to speak fluently in a language from the time period in which they claim to have lived. Hypnotherapist Dr. Harold Crasilneck tells of a hypnosis session where a woman began speaking in an ancient language and claimed to have lived in a town that existed centuries ago. Incredibly, both the language and the name of the town were later verified by scholars.[7]

Facts retrieved from past lives are discovered through either hypnotherapy or what is called spontaneous past-life recall. But, as we shall discover in the rest of this chapter, these methods are highly suspect.

SPONTANEOUS PAST-LIFE RECALL

Dr. Ian Stevenson, former head of the Department of Psychiatry of the Medical School of the University of Virginia, prefers to investigate those cases that are "suggestive" of reincarnation which come about "spontaneously" instead of those learned from hypnosis. His therapy usually involves a small child (two to four years of age) who has demonstrated knowledge and behavior corresponding to a person in a past life.

The child is usually taken "back" to where he lived in a past life. The accuracy rate of his knowledge of the deceased should be around 90 percent and there has to have been no verifiable way in which the child could have attained this knowledge through external means (parents, friends, books, etc.). The best quantitative and qualitative information comes from those children between the ages of three to five years old. Beyond this age range, memories and behavior begin to recede.

Stevenson interviews firsthand informants (parents, family members, neighbors, etc.), as well as the child. The quality of investigative evidence is undeniably questionable, especially when the investigator has only been on the scene of a small number of cases. And herein lies the problem with his method. John Hick (who is sympathetic with the doctrine of reincarnation) rightly criticizes Stevenson:

> But there is also invariably the defect, from the point of view of hard evidence, that no scientifically reliable investigation was made whilst the case was "raw" and before unconscious hints and clues, as well as errors in observation and almost inevitable exaggerations in the recounting of the tale, could have entered in. . . . These circumstances—and particularly the considerable lapse of time before Stevenson began his enquiries—reduce their evidential value, in my view, below the level at which they can properly be said to *prove* anything.[8]

After presenting his evidence for reincarnation, Stevenson himself states, "Neither any single case nor all of the investigated cases together offer anything like a proof of reincarnation."[9]

Also, Stevenson had assembled more than sixteen hundred cases of reincarnation types, most of which were from areas where there was a large belief in reincarnation. Naturally they would be susceptible to cultural conditioning.

Stevenson suggests that reincarnation may provide an explanation for unusual interests and activities shown by some children who do not remember anything about a previous life. For example, George Frederick Handel, the German-English composer *(Messiah)*, did not have any ancestors who had a talent in music; his father was sternly opposed to it and his mother was neutral. However, Stevenson notes that in the cases he has investigated it is regrettable that no empirical evidence has been found to substantiate the idea of reincarnation. No Western (or Indian) child prodigy has ever claimed to remember a previous life.

The theory of behaviorism claims that our behavior is *determined* (not just influenced) by external causes such as parental training, community expectations, and so forth. However, Stevenson is assuming that if we cannot discover any external modifying causes (influence of parents, traumatic experience, etc.) for a child's phobias, unusual interests, or behavior, then the explanation must come from a previous life.

Complete behaviorism proposes that no one can really freely choose to be a certain way; he is forced into behaving in a particular way by external forces. But if this is true, then why do behaviorists try to convince us to choose their position, when, in fact, their "doctrine" demands that we cannot choose anything—including behaviorism?

If complete behaviorism is true, then behaviorists are irrational because they did not rationally decide that behaviorism is true; they were conditioned to believe their theory by external forces (environment, genes, etc.).

If complete behaviorism is false, then there does not always have to be an external cause for thoughts, feelings, and behavior, and there is no need to look for an external cause in a previous life.

HYPNOTHERAPY

The use of hypnotherapy is also an inadequate method of finding evidence for reincarnation. Following are four reasons why this has been found to be so.

Hypnosis is dangerous. Past-life therapist Dick Sutphen thinks that the warnings about the dangers of hypnotic regression are absurd.

> They're [the medical community] threatened the moment they think anyone is taking away their thunder. They didn't even recognize that hypnosis existed until a few years ago and now they're trying to claim it for their own. . . . There's no difference between hypnosis and meditation or watching television or any other altered state of consciousness.[10]

Sutphen has even trained an estimated twenty-five thousand people to do past-lives regressions in a single five-day seminar. Yet paradoxically, Sutphen later turns around and says that "there are a lot of charlatans out there . . . and you can legislate against them, but it won't do a doggone thing. Anyone can buy a book and learn to hypnotize somebody."

In the same article Dr. Kenneth Altshuler, chairman of the psychiatry department at the University of Texas Health Science Center, said that "people tinker with their minds the way they never would with their bodies. . . . They seem to think one is more expendable than the other."

Cult expert Walter Martin warns that "sometimes when a person is regressed far enough back through his memory banks, an inexpert hypnotist may not be able to bring him back to the level at which he started."[11] Imagine being taken into a reality-distorted trance-state where you are separated from reality, *and then not being able to snap out of it!*

Hypnosis is deceptive. As Martin and Diedre Bobgan have pointed out, hypnosis is deceptive. "Even if a hypnotist attempts to make only true and honest statements, deception may enter in through the distortion of reality which begins during induction and continues throughout the hypnotic trance."[12]

The techniques which hypnotherapists use, such as repetition, deception, stimulation of the imagination, and emotionally-overtoned suggestions, effectively influence the will and response of the patient. The process of hypnosis is a type of manipulation. It leads "a person into a heightened state of suggestability—more simply, a condition in which one will believe almost anything," say the Bobgans. Some hypnotherapists unashamedly admit this fact. In *Psychology Today,* John S. Gillis said,

> Humanitarian fervor aside, it's the therapist's job to take power over the patient, push ahead with solving the problem, then convince the patient he or she is better, even if it means being devious.[13]

That hypnosis cannot make someone do something contrary to his will is really a misnomer. Dr. Bobgan notes that

> a hypnotist can even lead a person into committing murder by creating an extreme fear that someone is attempting to kill him. Through hypnotic deception, it is possible to cause one to do something against his will by disguising the act into one which would be within his choice.[14]

A hypnotherapist can manipulate the will of a person so as to deceive him into doing something immoral. Perhaps even more shockingly, she can make him forget that the act was even suggested. In the mid-nineteenth century, experiments on posthypnotic suggestions conducted by Liebault and Bernheim demonstrated that

> the hypnotherapist can give the subject a suggestion of something he will do after he is brought out of hypnosis, and then tell the subject that he will forget that the hypnotist has told him to perform the action. The patient will then not remember later the real cause of his posthypnotic behavior.[15]

Hypnosis is unreliable. Hypnosis is an unreliable source of information. For one thing, studies demonstrate that people are able and have been known to lie under hypnosis. It is also a known fact that memory is subject to distortion.

Hypnosis expert James E. Parejko in an article in the *Journal of the American Institute of Hypnosis* (January 1975) listed four factors of subconscious invention:

1. Expectations of the hypnotist/facilitator
2. Diminishment of critical thought in the mind of the sensor which accompanies deep trance states
3. A triggering idea by the facilitator
4. Hallucinating ability of the mind

All of these factors again demonstrate the danger of being unwillingly influenced by suggestions. Even the most careful hypnotist cannot help but influence the client under hypnosis. Bernard Diamond, a professor of law and clinical psychiatry, insists that the client cannot escape an increased state of suggestibility. Nor can she escape flights of fantasy, the lingering effects of suggestion from the hypnosis, or distinguish between fact and fantasy contained in the re-call.[16] While hypnosis is purported to be useful because it allows the client to ignore distractions and concentrate on a particular subject, it can also blend imagined events with real ones. The client can no longer discriminate between what he makes up and what actually happened.

In *Science* magazine, Kenneth Bowers, a psychologist at the University of Waterloo, Ontario, Canada, and Jane Dywan, a psychologist at McMaster University, reported

> that although hypnosis increases recall, it also increases errors. In their study, hypnotized subjects correctly recalled twice as many items as did unhypnotized members of a control group but also made three times as many mistakes. During hypnosis, you are creating memories.[17]

Another study published in *Science,* conducted by Campbell Perry and Jean-Roche Laurence, psychologists at Concordia University in Montreal, showed that under hypnosis, subjects are easily influenced by leading questions.

> The researchers asked a group of subjects to describe the events of a particular night. After making sure that the subjects had no specific memories of that night, the psychologists put them under hypnosis and asked them if they had heard a noise that woke them up. Thirteen out of twenty-seven subjects reported hearing something. Some were so certain that they still claimed to have heard the sounds even after they were told that the hypnotist had suggested it.[18]

One of the problems with advocates of hypnosis is that they are assuming a "videotape theory" of memory. However, the "reconstructive theory" of memory is probably a more accurate description of true memory. In other words, people's memories under hypnosis can be altered as well as changed by subtle cues from the hypnotist.

No wonder courts are now leery of using hypnosis as a basis for evidence. In certain cases in the past, criminals were identified solely through hypnosis. But this no longer seems to be a viable option. The California Supreme Court decided that "the memory does not act like a videotape recorder, but rather is subject to numerous influences that continuously alter its contents."[19]

Investigators in an Illinois case suggested to a witness that he could "zoom in" under hypnosis on the facial features of a man who had been 273 feet away, with a street lamp as the only source of light. Under those conditions, opthalmologists testified that it would be impossible to identify a face at more than 30 feet. It comes as no surprise then that "at least thirteen states now have some sort of restriction concerning the use of hypnosis to obtain eyewitness testimony, and the current trend is toward more stringent rulings."[20]

Hypnosis has close parallels with the Eastern occultism. Professor of psychology Charles Tart experimented with a well-adjusted twenty-year-old college student whom he called William, taking him through various levels of hypnosis.

> At deeper levels there is an awareness of some sort of chant or humming sound that is identified with the feeling that more and more experience is potentially available. . . . The chant William reported may be related to the Hindu concept of the sacred syllable Om,

supposedly a basic sound of the universe that a man can "hear" as mind becomes more universally attuned.[21]

As Tart moved William into various levels of hypnosis, William's experiences were

> similar to Eastern descriptions of consciousness of the void . . . in which time, space, and ego are supposedly transcended, leaving pure awareness of the primal nothingness from which all manifested creation comes.[22]

Erika Fromm claims that the state of hypnosis is identical to that of an altered state of consciousness. This condition is no different from a mystical, out-of-the-body experience where the passage of time becomes meaningless.

In his book *Principles of Spiritual Hypnosis* Peter Francuch affirms that there is a trance-level of hypnosis corresponding to the state of void or nirvana experienced by the Eastern mystics. No words to describe this experience exist in our vocabulary.

Hypnosis expert William Kroger states that "for centuries, Zen, Buddhist, Tibetan, and Yogic methods have used a system of meditation and an altered state of consciousness similar to hypnosis."[23] He says that although there are supposed differences between Zen, Yoga, and other Eastern healing methodologies, they are fundamentally the same.

SUMMARY

We might ask our reincarnationist friends why it is that most do not remember their previous incarnations if in fact reincarnation is true. They probably would respond in four ways.[24]

1. *Physical birth* is such a violent event that it shatters one's memories of previous lives. Thus, past-life recall is the exception to the rule.
2. *The subconscious* is known to store data which most do not recall. Perhaps here is where the knowledge of past lives is stored. This is supposedly confirmed by the fact that being put into a trance seems to release what is in the subconscious, often revealing past lives.
3. *The nature of memory* is such that people have a difficult time remembering their infant life and childhood. How much more so, it is argued, that a life before infancy and birth would be difficult to remember.
4. *A hindrance to moral growth* would arise if one was to remember his past deeds. (This response will be evaluated in chapter 7.)

All of these responses are less than satisfactory. They cannot be disproved, nor can they be verified. Even though someone may have knowledge of a personality who lived in a past era does not necessarily mean he actually was that person. Furthermore, the means by which this knowledge of the past is gained, namely by spontaneous past-life recall and hypnotherapy, are dubious at best, and at worst, diabolical.

Is all hypnotism occult? Hypnosis may not be inherently occult, but it certainly places the client in a "passively receptive state" which could open the door to adverse spiritual influences. The Bobgans advise that Christians should avoid hypnosis because of its apparent occult nature and because it is practiced by many who are involved in the occult.

To conclude this chapter on psychology and reincarnation, the arguments from the field of psychology fail to demonstrate the reality of reincarnation. And even if reincarnation were true, it would infer some disturbing implications, which we will look at in the next chapter. We now turn to the task of considering alternative explanations for the data which are mistakenly interpreted as evidences suggestive of reincarnation.

C H A P T E R 5
ALTERNATIVE EXPLANATIONS

In the last chapter, we unearthed the problems of trying to prove reincarnation with evidences from hypnotherapy and spontaneous past-life recall. What are some alternative explanations? Before we take a look at these alternatives, it should be noted that the whole matter of trying to prove a past existence based on past-life recall assumes that a person actually *had to be there* in order to have that knowledge.

But as John Snyder has shown in his book *Reincarnation vs. Resurrection,* citing the example of psychic Peter Hurkos, the knowledge of past events does not imply *presence* in those events. Peter Hurkos recollected data of past events with an astonishing 87–99 percent accuracy rate. According to the argument from the knowledge of past facts, Hurkos could be considered as someone who is recalling his past lives. He knows of events in the past before his birth; therefore, according to reincarnationists, he *lived through* those events. But Hurkos also displayed traits which are contrary to reincarnation theory.

His knowledge of past lives also encompassed events which took place after his birth! This obviously was not a case of remembering a "past life." Moreover, he "remembered" lives of two or more persons who lived simultaneously and even some phrases of the languages they spoke. Common sense tells us that one cannot be reincarnated in two or more people at the same time. Therefore, while it cannot be charged that Hurkos's case is contrary to reincarnation theory—so that all past-life recallers are false, it can be argued that this case demonstrates how one can have accurate knowledge of past events without actually having been there.

In order for past-life recall to be used as support for reincarnation, one must prove that knowledge of certain events implies being present at those events. This reasoning would lead one to believe that since Hurkos "recalled" past events, he must have been there. But we have already shown that this was impossible in Hurkos's case. Therefore, Hurkos knew past events without having lived them out. And once the reincarnationist admits that one could have knowledge of past events without having been there, his case for reincarnation is greatly weakened.

It has also been argued that "memories" cannot prove reincarnation since memories can be programmed into computers. Given our technology today, it is not far-fetched to think that we could devise a machine that would record the memories of one person (Marilyn) and feed them into another (Bob). In this situation, the memories of Marilyn and Bob would be identical. But Bob is obviously not an incarnation of Marilyn. The point is that reincarnation is not automatically proved just because of identical or similar memories. Human personhood involves more than mere memories; it is a composite of memories, emotions, personality, intelligence, and so forth (even a body).

Then how can we account for this amazing phenomenon of identical or very similar memories without believing in reincarnation? Following are four alternative explanations for so-called past-life recall.

ALTERNATIVE EXPLANATIONS

FRAUD

Many cases thought to have been authentic examples of past-life recall (and thus, reincarnation) have later turned out to be fraudulent. The famous Bridey Murphy case (see *The Search for Bridey Murphy*) was debunked by further research.[1] Through hypnosis, a woman supposedly regressed to old Ireland in the seventeenth or eighteenth century. She reportedly spoke Gaelic, described the coastline where she lived, discussed many of the customs and clothing, and even had a deep Irish accent. But it was later revealed that Bridey Murphy never existed at all but was a figment of a child's imagination. This woman was reared by her grandmother, who spoke Gaelic and who had history books about old Ireland. These books had been read by the little girl, and her grandmother had taught her Gaelic. Apparently, she had forgotten the language and the history books as she grew older; but they were never totally erased from her memory. The facts of past events locked away in her subconscious arose under hypnosis. However, while many other cases have also been proven to be fraudulent in nature, whether intentional or not, fraud does not explain all cases of past-life recall.

CRYPTOAMNESIA

Have you ever found yourself in the middle of a conversation and had the uncanny feeling that the event had taken place before? Or walked into a room where you had never been and felt an odd sense that you had been there before? This is often called *déjà vu* (French for "already seen"). Scientists

75

tell us that this is a form of "cryptoamnesia"; that is, a process whereby a person forgets that she got her information from a past source (in her present life) and comes to believe that this information is a memory from a previous existence.

Dr. Maurice S. Rawlings, associate clinical professor of medicine at the University of Tennessee, says there are times when the subconscious relates a present event with a previous one that the conscious mind does not remember.[2] We think that we had been in a certain conversation before, when in actuality the present conversation is so much like a conversation we had in the past (i.e., same topic, atmosphere, etc.) that our minds fuse them together.

Researchers have found a possible physiological basis for *déjà vu*. When data from the environment enters the eye, sometimes the transmission of this information to the brain is delayed for a micro-second; this leads the person to believe that she had seen it before. But again, this alternative explanation to reincarnation cannot account for all cases of past-life recall.

CULTURAL CONDITIONING

Many forces in our environment influence our beliefs and values. We have all experienced and have seen children experience the tendency to submit to peer pressure. Many of the accounts of past-life recall can be attributed to this factor. As Indian parapsychologist and past-life researcher C. T. K. Chari says,

> It is disconcerting to learn that, out of some 300 alleged cases [of past-life recall], over 100 are from India. Can we ignore a cultural predisposition to interpret the facts in accordance with a myth-motif? . . . An al-

leged universal law of rebirth which is so highly conditioned by purely local factors is suspect.[3]

Past-life recalls often take place in a culture which is conducive to the belief in reincarnation. Dr. Ian Stevenson, perhaps the most respected researcher of "cases suggestive of reincarnation," admits that

> the principal sites of abundant reported cases are: northern India; Sri Lanka; Burma; Thailand; Vietnam; western Asia, especially south central Turkey, Lebanon, and Syria; and northwest North America, among the natives of that region. The peoples of these areas (of the groups among whom the cases occur) believe in reincarnation.[4]

Dr. Stevenson's cases have been found primarily in certain areas of India, where the belief in reincarnation is prominent, particularly in Uttar Pradesh, where the belief in reincarnation is more firmly held than in other areas of India. The belief in reincarnation persists strongly among the Druses in Lebanon and Syria, where the incidence of cases is perhaps the highest in the world. Parents have little or no objection to claims made by children to remember a previous life. In Brazil the widespread belief of reincarnation has also created a cultural climate favorable to past-life recall cases. Children who make assertions of previous lives have the respect of their parents.

Consequently we should not belittle the influence of the environment on the subconscious or unconscious mind, especially when most of the spontaneous past-life recall cases come from children. This alternative is one of the best explanations for so-called past-life recalls and perhaps accounts for the great majority of cases. However, in all fairness to Stevenson and others, past-life recalls do occur (however rarely) outside of cultures that advocate the doctrine of reincarnation. Cultural conditioning cannot explain the rare cases of past-life recall we have yet to investigate. These other cases seem to involve "higher powers."

DEMONIC POSSESSION

Scripture affirms the reality of demonic oppression/possession (Matt. 8:28-33; Luke 4:33-36; Acts 16:16-18; 19:11-16). Could the influence of demons explain the incredible cases of past-life recall?

Morris Netherton recorded a possible proof for reincarnation of several independent but almost identical past-life recalls. These covered a period of several years and were from people who did not know each other but who claimed to have witnessed a crucifixion account which differed from that in the Gospels.[5]

Following is an account of the cases in the order they occurred:

- *April 1970:* A young man claimed to have been a disciple of Jesus. As he ran to where Jesus was being crucified he was clobbered on the head by one of the guards. About forty other men were being executed as well. When he revived, he heard the other disciples say, "What do we do now?"
- *1983:* Another patient experienced a past-life recall, where, as a child, he witnessed forty men being executed. He also remembered a man running toward one of the crosses and being struck on his head by one of the soldiers.
- *8 months later:* A woman saw a vision of forty crosses as well as an agitated man getting hit on his head.

- *1 year later:* A woman recollected being a nine-year-old girl who wandered into a cave where she heard one of the disciples say, "What do we do now?" She also saw a man stumble in with a head wound.
- *Sometime later:* During a past-life recall, a man saw himself in a pile of about forty dead men. Like the rest of them, he too was crucified. As the guards ran them through, he heard them talking about the "Jew" who was taken away by his disciples. In their conversation, the guards mentioned a man who they had to pop on the head because he had run up to one of the crosses.

For those of us who believe the biblical accounts there is no difficulty in accepting the possibility of a demonic cause for these supernormal events. De Arteaga, himself an advocate of past-life visions, discerningly notes that Netherton ignores a possible demonic source in these cases.

Edgar Cayce, a prophet of reincarnationism, considered the possibility of demonic influence in his "revelations."

> That's what I always thought, and against this I put the idea that the Devil might be tempting me to do his work by operating through me when I was conceited enough to think God had given me special power. . . . If ever the Devil was going to play a trick on me, this would be it.[6]

In his book *Reincarnation: A Christian Appraisal* Mark Albrecht has speculated as to how a demon might produce a past-life recall. He reasons that if what Nobel laureate Sir John Eccles once said was true, namely, that "the brain is a machine that a ghost can operate," then perhaps a demonic spirit could replace a person's control over his own mind and body. Demonic spirits have accumulated data spanning thousands of years and are capable of plugging this information into the mind of the one being influenced. Albrecht suggests that demons could tap into a kind of spiritual data bank for information.

Stevenson argues that there is a difference between cases of possession and those suggestive of reincarnation. With the former, the personality is transformed; but with the latter, this is not always the situation. Chari charges that this is a futile distinction since, at times, even trained observers cannot detect the shifts in personality with classical cases of multiple personalities. In some cases, Stevenson's subjects remembered the exact locations of where their bodies were hidden or buried. However, a reincarnated person would have no memory of these kinds of facts.[7]

De Arteaga confesses, "In reference to the demonic counterfeit hypothesis, we can safely say that for many PLVs [past-life visions] it is the most solidly verified hypothesis of all."[8] Thus, whereas fraud, cryptoamnesia, and even cultural conditioning cannot account for those rare, yet detailed, past-life recalls, demonism can.

DO SPIRIT GUIDES
CONFIRM REINCARNATION?

Through the use of seances and mediums, spirit guides (presumed to be the souls of the deceased) are said to affirm the truth of reincarnation, often revealing the "past lives" of others.

Elisabeth Kübler-Ross began her work with dying patients and soon moved on to work in the area of life beyond death. Through her studies, she came to embrace the doctrine of reincarnation, her spirit guides confirming her new belief. They told her that God desires all people to be present with him at the end of one lifetime, but that this is not always possible. Some are in need of many reincarnations, having to spend as many as two million years on earth before they are able to become a spirit.[9]

The Bible says:

> Do not turn to mediums or spiritists; do not seek them out to be defiled by them. I am the Lord your God (Lev. 19:31).
>
> And when they say to you, "Consult the mediums and the spiritists who whisper and mutter," should not a people consult their God? Should they consult the dead on behalf of the living? (Isa. 8:19; see also 1 Sam. 28:7-19 and 1 Chron. 10:13).
>
> When you enter the land which the Lord your God gives you, you shall not learn to imitate the detestable things of those nations. There shall not be found among you . . . a medium, or a spiritist, or one who calls up the dead. For whoever does these things is detestable to the Lord; and because of these detestable things the Lord your God will drive them out before you. . . . For those nations, which you shall dispossess, listen to those who practice witchcraft and to diviners, but as for you, the Lord your God has not allowed you to do so (Deut. 18:9-12, 14).

Scripture makes it clear that any attempt to contact the dead is an abomination to God. Robert A. Morey, in *Death and the Afterlife,* lists three other scriptural arguments against consulting the dead:

- Consulting mediums warranted the death penalty (Lev. 20:27).

- Consulting mediums was connected with astrology and human sacrifice (2 Kings 21:5, 6).
- Consulting mediums arose in a time of rebellion and idolatry; it disappeared in time of renewal and restoration of Israel (2 Kings 23:24).

Most importantly, the Bible makes it clear that consulting mediums makes one vulnerable to demonic deception (Deut. 18:11; 1 Tim. 4:1).

DO BIRTHMARKS PROVE REINCARNATION?

Does being born with unusual birthmarks around the neck and wrists suggest that a person might be the reincarnation of an early American slave who was chained to his quarters? Some reincarnationists argue that because a living individual bears the same unique physical marks as a deceased individual, he therefore could be a reincarnation of the deceased.

These unique physical characteristics are not limited to mere moles; some of them include major congenital malformations such as greatly deformed limbs or even complete absence of fingers, toes, or hands. But how is "uniqueness" to be proven? And why are only some features carried on to the next incarnation to the exclusion of others? Certainly the demonic must be considered as a possible source.

In some cases, as with the Lakhers of Assam, marks are deliberately made on the corpses of children during the burial while the parents entreat their offspring to come back to them. When a newborn infant is said to bear marks which are similar to those on a corpse, the Lakhers claim this is a case of reincarnation. But if this were so, how could a corpse bear the "karmic energy" to be transferred to its next incarnation? Once the person is dead, her soul is believed to have already left the body.

SOME DISTURBING IMPLICATIONS OF THE DOCTRINE OF REINCARNATION

We have looked at the major arguments for reincarnation in the area of psychological evidence. All of the arguments have been shown to be inadequate. Before we go on to the next chapter, let's look at some implications of believing in reincarnation doctrine.

EXPLAINS AUTISM?

In his article, "The Exploratory Value of the Idea of Reincarnation," Stevenson proposes that reincarnation could explain autism without looking to the parents (as is commonly done) for possible causes. In many autistic cases, it has been proven that it is not the result of parental rejection of the child but the child's rejection of parental affection at infancy. Stevenson suggests that perhaps such rejection derives from unhappy experiences with the parents in a previous life.

EXPLAINS PREGNANCY CRAVINGS?

Stevenson also states that when a pregnant woman shows a craving (or perhaps aversion) for a particular food, it could be explained by a previous life of the child she is carrying who also craved or had an aversion to certain foods.

JUSTIFIABLE PARENT SWITCHING?

Children expressing belief in being a reincarnation of a previous person sometimes express desires to be with their former parents. In her book, *Voices from Home,* actress Anne Francis talked about an occasion when her younger daughter told her she was different from all the other mommies she had ever had before.

DELUSIONS OF GRANDEUR?

Werner Erhard, the founder of est, once queried, "How do you know I'm not the reincarnation of Jesus Christ? You wouldn't believe the feelings I have inside me."[10]

REVENGE?

One of the cases which Brad Steiger presents as a showcase of reincarnation experiences concerns a go-go dancer in an Indiana nightclub who swears that she is a reincarnation of an ancient temple love goddess. She believes that she was terribly abused by a high priest who lowered her position to that of a temple prostitute. When she refused to surrender her body to a group of drunken men in accordance with her "oath of love," they viciously violated her body to the point of death. She told Steiger, "I know that the high priest has also been reincarnated. . . . I am seeking him out to kill him."[11] Even in Stevenson's findings several children have spoken openly about taking revenge on their assailants when they became big enough to do so.

GROUNDS FOR DIVORCE?

Mary Lynn had three past-life regressions done in which her ex-husband played a role.

> Once I was married to him but very much in love with another man, and my husband killed my lover. . . . In another lifetime, I watched him drown and didn't try to save him. And in another life, he was my father and abandoned me.[12]

GROUNDS FOR MARRIAGE?

Brad Steiger reports an incident that happened to a football player. During a college football game, Martin J. cracked his ribs and blacked out. He then had a vision of a pretty black-haired girl who laughed at him and said, "Clumsy, you should be more careful. I'm just going to have to look after you." When he opened his eyes a couple of the guys helped him off the field. The next day Martin's girlfriend took him to the hospital for X rays. As he was walking down the hallway he saw a nurse coming toward him that looked very familiar. He walked right into a water cooler and fell down. The nurse looked down at him and said, "Clumsy, you should be more careful. I guess I'll just have to walk along with you and look after you." Martin talked an intern into getting rid of his girlfriend while he made a date with the nurse. They planned to be married after graduation.

CONFUSED SEXUALITY?

Some of Stevenson's subjects who claim to be the reincarnation of a deceased person have openly expressed "sexual aspirations" for that person's wife (or husband).

CONFUSED GENDER (HOMOSEXUALITY)?

Some subjects of Stevenson's research have included those claiming to remember a previous life as a person of the opposite sex. The subject usually expresses traits characteristic of the opposite sex, such as partiality for the clothes and activities of the opposite sex. Shirley MacLaine discovered that reincarnation provided her with an explanation which led to her acceptance of homosexuality. One of her psychic mentors explained that the sexual preference of such individuals plays an important part in the requirement for understanding that we are all basically the same because we have all experienced being both sexes; our souls, if you will, are basically androgynous.[13]

SUMMARY

To conclude this chapter, we have noted that there are alternative explanations for cases of past-life recall and assertions of previous lives. There have been past-life recalls that were thought to be legitimate but which later turned out to be fraudulent. Others can be attributed to cryptoamnesia or cultural conditioning. And, of course, we cannot deny the possibility of the demonic as a source for the supernormal events in these past-life recall cases. Further, if reincarnation were true, it would imply some disturbing consequences, including the justification of homosexuality, divorce, and even murder.

CHAPTER 6
JUSTICE AND REINCARNATION

An exam is blown, and with it the hopes of a higher grade point average. "Should I have taken that job?" "Why didn't I go out with him; he might have become a good friend . . . lover? Perhaps even, . . . a lifetime mate?" We all feel that there were times when we might have done something other than what we chose to do. If only we had another chance! If only we could do it all over again! Missed opportunities. Deep, searing scars of regret. Life seems so unfair. Would not a loving and just God give us another chance at life?

Many reincarnationists argue that in order for there to be justice and love in the cosmos, God must give us a second chance. In this chapter, we will look at arguments which discuss the issues of justice and reincarnation.

THE LOVE OF GOD
DEMANDS REINCARNATION

"One of the most attractive aspects of reincarnation is that it removes entirely the possibility of damnation," writes Quincy Howe.[1] John Hick finds the doctrine of eternal torment, where a conscious creature must endure physical and mental torture throughout unending time, as "horrible and disturbing beyond words." Such a conception is "totally incompatible with the idea of God as infinite love." Hick wonders how justice could ever demand the "infinite penalty of eternal pain" for "finite human sins."[2] In short, if God is all-loving, then he will not send anyone to hell.

Geddes MacGregor, in his book *Reincarnation in Christianity*, says that it is intolerable to think "that even one sinner should be punished by everlasting torture." The fundamental Christian belief that God is love does not seem compatible with the belief in eternal punishment of the unsaved.

Howe declares that such a position is

> abhorrent to anyone who sees God's love as perfect and all-embracing. Although the fundamentalists still preach eternal damnation, more liberal Christianity is moving towards a view in which God's forgiveness will finally take in all creatures.[3]

These writers are suggesting that the love of God demands the doctrine of universalism. That is, that *everyone without exception* (some include the Devil here) will eventually be saved. In other words, there is no hell.

How could an all-loving God assign infinite consequences to the moral choices of "just" one lifetime? Surely God will give us all a second chance! Reincarnation, according to these enthusiasts, best models such a "loving" attitude. After all, who could continue to obstinately and persistently resist the redeeming love of God when confronted with the lamentable results? Frederick Spencer finds it inconceivable that any rational being would "reject eternal happiness for an eternity of comparative unhappiness." Only irrational, and therefore irresponsible, people would make such a choice. For Spencer, this exceptional case would justly warrant God's working to change this person in a supernatural way "without the overriding of his freedom, inasmuch as his freedom would no longer exist." Yes, free choice "is mighty, but the love of God is mightier."[4]

The reincarnationist believes in a cosmic moral law and the ultimate triumph of righteousness but denies Jesus' teaching that the consequence of evil deeds is *eternal* punishment and therefore unredemptive suffering. There is judgment, but only intermediate judgment (spread out through many lifetimes), not ultimate judgment. In order to substantiate this claim, Hick refers us to 1 Corinthians 15:22 and Romans 5:18 where Paul parallels a universal fall in Adam with a universal restoration in Christ. He also cites Romans 11:32, Ephesians 1:10, and 1 Timothy 2:4 and asserts that the New Testament testifies to "the final salvation of all men and indeed to the restoration of the entire created order."[5]

Yet Hick recognizes that we could also quote passages of Paul that would argue *against* universalism (cf. Rom. 9, 2 Thess. 1:8, 9). However, Hick maintains that at times the inner logic of Paul's writings on "the saving activity of God . . . inevitably unfolded itself into the thought of universal salvation." In other words, Paul may not have been aware of the full implications of his teachings which, according to Hick, proclaim universalism.

Lynn de Silva likewise asserts that the idea of endless torment after death is mainly due to literalist distortions of such terms as "the unquenchable fire," "hades," "Sheol," "paradise," "Abraham's bosom," "heaven," etc.—all relics of an archaic cosmology.[6]

Hick claims that these two so-called "biblical" ideas are

not contradictory: "Unless you repent, you will surely perish" and "in the end all will turn from their wickedness and live." These statements are compatible when they are understood in this way: *If* we don't repent, then we'll die in hell; *but* everyone *will eventually repent!*

In other words, the unrepentance that leads to damnation is *hypothetically* true, but *actually* false. Eternal damnation is what could happen if we do not repent; but all will repent. Thus, the theologian is "speaking logically about God" when he infers, on the basis of divine love and power, that in the end God will succeed in saving all his human creatures. Hence, we must "affirm the ultimate salvation of all mankind; and the faith in which we affirm this is that in which we have affirmed God's saving love and sovereign power."[7]

Even "Christian" reincarnationists who reject universalism stress the need for a second chance. Whether in this world or another, they insist, we simply need more time to work out our salvation. Thus,

> the notion of second chance (or, better, of a series of chances) is one that accords with what is to be expected by those who accept the biblical revelation that God's ways, however mysterious, are in the long run seen to be compassionate and morally constructive.[8]

MacGregor states that now we can understand the ancient doctrine of purgatory which expresses the "pilgrimage of purification and growth" that appropriately fits us for the future life. He uses a classroom analogy to illustrate this point: Just as students are often given a second chance to resit an examination, so a God of love would not deny us a chance to try again when we fail to finish within the time allotted.

MacGregor sees "no reason why a Christian should not at least entertain the suggestion that the re-embodiment [reincarnation] should occur over and over again, giving the individual opportunity to grow in the love of God." In fact, MacGregor is inclined to believe that "the concept of reincarnation is, indeed, the key to a fuller Christian understanding of human destiny."[9] Since it is man's purpose in life to trust in Christ he will go on being reborn until eventually he fulfills that purpose. For de Arteaga, reincarnation does not imply universal salvation but merely universal proclamation of the gospel. Hence, a "Christian" view of reincarnation would imply "that sooner or later *everyone* will have an opportunity to accept the gospel before the Last Judgment."[10]

MORAL PERFECTION CANNOT BE REACHED WITHOUT REINCARNATION

The process of sanctification (the process toward increased holiness of the Christian after having been justified by Christ) is a gradual one; and so, argue reincarnationists, it implies the need for more than one lifetime. Many reincarnationists assume the truth of evolution. Just as there is physical evolution in the cosmos, so there is moral evolution in the universe.

Even though Spencer admits that some phases of physical evolution appeared quite rapidly, to understand such a leap in the moral sphere from our present depravity to the holiness of God seems unintelligible. "At death man is not automatically transformed into a perfect being. He must grow into perfection. He must be transformed 'from one degree of glory to another' " (2 Cor. 3:18).[11]

Christians should "expect a long evolutionary, purgatorial process. The task is not only too complex and too arduous to be quickly accomplished; it is of such a nature that setbacks are to be expected."[12] According to Mac-Gregor, as well as other reincarnationists, there are many purgatories, and one is earth. The attainment of perfection entails a tremendous amount of effort and time—perhaps billions of years. Continual embodiment must take place, again and again, until "the gold is all sifted out from the dross."[13]

> It follows that responsible life must continue beyond bodily death. . . . Life is thus aptly imaged in terms of the ancient picture of an arduous journey toward the life of the Celestial City. This pilgrimage crosses the frontier of death; for its end is not attained in this life, and therefore, if it is to be attained at all, there must be a further life, or lives, in which God's purpose continues to hold us in being in environments related to that purpose.[14]

JUSTICE DEMANDS REINCARNATION

E. D. Walker in his book *Reincarnation: A Study of Forgotten Truth* declares, "The strongest support of reincarnation is its happy solution of the problem of moral inequality and injustice and evil which otherwise overwhelms us as we survey the world." This argument is interwoven with the doctrine of karma, the moral law governing man's destiny. Although one of the deepest theological problems besetting Christianity is the problem of suffering, the belief in reincarnation provides a "more rational and satisfying answer" to this problem than the belief in one life on earth followed by heaven or hell thereafter.

Biblical literature confirms the fact that "the wicked *do* flourish and the righteous *are* and *remain* the victims of appalling injustice in this life" (see Job 12:6; 21:7-9; Ps. 73:3-4, 12; Eccles. 8:14; Jer. 12:1). Reincarnation presents a serious proposal as to how these inequities could be rectified in the course of millions, perhaps trillions, of years, if not at the next turn of the wheel of rebirth. Howe asks,

> How are we to believe in a perfect and loving God if he persistently seems to place man in tragic and painful situations? What can the Christian pastor say to the mother of a defective child? Only that the counsels of God are hidden from man, as that he may learn to grow in faith. What of the millions of all ages who are daily dying of starvation? Lacking a direct and reasonable explanation for this, even the most faithful Christian is occasionally tempted to hold God responsible. It is indeed an exacting and hard test of faith for man to affirm the goodness of God while surrounded by misery and suffering.[15]

The reincarnationist attempts to resolve the perplexing problem of evil with the logic of karma. The law of karma entirely absolves God of the responsibility for human suffering, and man takes total responsibility for his life.

Thus the reincarnationist explains the problem of moral injustice and human suffering. Since our God is a God of justice, he would not allow someone to suffer except as a consequence of sins. Children who suffer illness and death and who obviously could not have committed any sins in their lifetime are atoning for sins committed during a previous existence.

Accordingly, Howe claims that every circumstance in which a man finds himself can ultimately be traced back to his karma. MacGregor also asserts the biblical idea of "we reap what we sow" (Mark 4:13-20; 2 Cor. 9:6; Ps.

126:5, 6) and tells us that cruelty and injustice will "catch up with the perpetrator sooner or later; perhaps in the next lifetime, perhaps only after many lifetimes."[16] Likewise, goodness will not fail to follow one through his series of lives.

But despite MacGregor's protest that karma should not be taken to the exclusion of "the operation of divine mercy such as is at the heart of the gospel message," he fails to demonstrate how this is possible. He insists that the law of karma is

> inseparable from the divine benevolence and love at its source. . . . Karma is . . . itself gracious. God's justice and God's mercy work together. In the operation of the karmic law we are not punished as by an angry dictator or vengeful conqueror. On the contrary, we are corrected as by a loving parent.[17]

A further argument for the compatibility of reincarnation with the Christian faith is the light it sheds on the doctrine of original sin. The traditional understanding of this doctrine where Adam is responsible for our sin is considered merely a "makeshift of the theologians." The theory of "a hereditary depravity" grates against the common sense of mankind for justice demands that only the individual himself can be blamed for his own wrongdoing. Hence, "the only satisfactory theory traces its beginning to earlier lives."[18]

Thus, in light of reincarnation, the doctrine of original sin is made intelligible by realizing that "each is his own Adam or her own Eve: each suffers as each has personally *chosen* to suffer after reflection on failures and the demands of personal dignity."[19]

SALVATION IS BEST EXPLAINED
IN TERMS OF REINCARNATION

Reincarnationists believe that hell is done away with, or at least, postponed. The way to perfection lies on a path that is painstakingly slow and arduous because karma must be worked out by the individual through many lives. How then is salvation understood by the "Christian" reincarnationist? What does the work of Christ accomplish?

According to the reincarnationist, Christ liberates us from the burden of our sins, the guilt of which would block our progress. MacGregor calls Christ the "perfect catalyst," the provider of "the conditions that make possible [a person's] salvation."[20]

"Man himself must make his peace with God." Howe contends that the vicarious atonement—Christ's substitutionary death on the cross for our sins—has been done away with. Salvation is not acquired by trusting in the completed work of Christ, but by using the work of Christ to complete our own salvation.

Jesus is no longer conceived of as being "the savior who delivers from damnation, but rather is the one who provides through his life and unfailing help vivid assurances of God's love." Despite this, Howe assures us that "the message of Christ's ministry and his suffering on the cross are in no way minimized for the reincarnationist." The cross is viewed solely as the price Christ was willing to pay in order to assure men of the love of God. "To be saved by Christ means to know that one stands in the unfailing light of God's love."[21]

According to the reincarnationist, the death of Christ does not satisfy God's demands for the punishment of sin. Christ's death only makes more conducive the conditions in which *we* must satisfy the penal demands of the law and appease the wrath of God. Reincarnationist atonement is thus centered in the self. For the law of karma rules that we have made ourselves what we are by former actions, and we are building our future eternity by present actions. Walker states:

> There is no destiny but what we ourselves determine. There is no salvation or condemnation except what we ourselves bring about. God places all the powers of the universe at our disposal, and the handle by which we use them to construct our fate has been and is and always shall be our own individual will.[22]

MacGregor concurs, stating that individual responsibility for one's own salvation logically follows from the notion of karma. "My karma is particular to *me*. It is *my* problem and the triumph over it is *my* triumph." We cannot escape the fact that

> man will have to achieve this transformation himself, for there is no other way in which any progress, not least any moral progress, can be made. Yet of course the Christian good news is that while without the redeeming work of Christ we could not hope to accomplish that self-transformation of humanity, with Christ we can and we shall.[23]

Like the Torah, the karmic law was fulfilled, not destroyed, by Jesus Christ. Divine grace, divine providence, and redemption through Christ all operate in, with, and through the karmic law. Hence, the karmic law does not exclude grace and redemption any more than does the Torah to which Jesus was referring. . . . Grace gives me a unique opportunity; it puts me in a privileged position by providing conditions of unheard-of advantage; but it no more erases the law than my good fortune in having a good teacher absolves me from the need to learn.[24]

Good teachers help us to learn, they do not do our homework. Karma teaches us that only evil is reaped from evil and good from good. It therefore teaches us that we need the grace of God and the work of Christ to provide the conditions by which we can work off our karmic debt, since without these conditions our moral progress would be greatly impeded.

SUMMARY

We conclude this chapter by noting that reincarnationists claim that reincarnation best reveals the love of God by giving humanity many opportunities for salvation and freedom to attain perfection through evolutionary development. They believe that reincarnation provides the only satisfactory answer to the compatibility of an all-loving, all-powerful God with evil and suffering in the world. Finally, according to reincarnationists, Christ is viewed as the catalyst providing the inspiration to motivate an individual as he continues on his journey toward God working out his own salvation.

It is proposed by "Christian" reincarnationists that the doctrine of reincarnation is not only necessitated by a sense of justice, but is also compatible with Christianity. In the next two chapters we will evaluate these arguments.

CHAPTER 7
THE INJUSTICE OF REINCARNATION

Is life without reincarnation unjust? Why is one born into the lap of luxury while another is thrust into a miserable existence of poverty and pain? How do we reconcile the apparent injustices in the world? Some people are naturally intelligent or athletic, others have no presence of mind or physical abilities. Are these "inequities" a thorn in the side of traditional Christianity? Does the problem of evil militate against the thought of a personal, all-loving, and all-powerful God?

In this chapter and the next we will look at the arguments presented in the last chapter which attempted to demonstrate the validity and reality of the doctrine of reincarnation. But before we do, let's take some time here to note some of the positive contributions that reincarnationists have to offer.

First, they commendably point out the need for more discussion on the subject of life after death. It is difficult to understand why there is such a vacuum of material on the afterlife in Christian literature when the hope of our salvation is directly connected with life after death (1 Cor. 15:12-19).

Second, they desire to protect the love, mercy, and justice

of God in the face of an evil world. Recognizing the tension which confronts anyone who would dare to proclaim the benevolence of God from the mountaintop of despair, they attempt to render the relationship between God and the existence of evil more intelligible.

Third, their emphasis on morality leads them to preserve the dignity of human beings and the love of God by retaining free will and responsibility as important elements of their belief. In order to be a moral being, a person must be free to choose either good or evil—free to choose to rely solely on the grace of God for one's salvation and enablement to do good works.

Despite these valuable contributions, there are some fundamental criticisms which can be leveled at those who believe in reincarnation. In this section, we shall show that their arguments are ill-founded. The following critique is far from exhaustive, but thorough enough to demonstrate the falsity of reincarnation as well as the *incompatibility* of it with the Christian faith. It should be noted that not all of these criticisms apply to all of the reincarnation models presented.

KARMA DOES NOT SOLVE
THE PROBLEM OF EVIL

As we have seen, the doctrine of reincarnation relies on the doctrine of karma. Even "Christian" reincarnationists cannot totally escape this ancient belief. Despite their timidity toward this Eastern doctrine, they all affirm in some sense that past lives influence or determine future ones. Even in Hick's case, where there are no past lives from one's existence on earth, he assumes that one's conduct in the present life on earth influences his next incarnation in other worlds. This is essentially the Eastern doctrine of karma.

Our first response to the reincarnational or karmic solution to the problem of evil is that we find it repulsive to our moral sensitivities. It "solves" the dilemma of the innocent suffering by saying that anyone who suffers is not innocent. Likewise, it attempts to solve the dilemma of the righteous suffering by saying that anyone who suffers is not righteous. In short, they are not *resolving* the issue; they are simply *dismissing* it.

The doctrine of karma not only grates against our sense of justice, it contradicts reason as well. To begin with, it seems unjust for God to punish children for the sins of adults; especially when these children do not remember "their" sins. In the tenth century A.D., when the doctrine of transmigration was gaining ground among Jews of the Karaite sect and certain Muslims attempted to reconcile this Eastern doctrine with their respective sacred writings (the Old Testament and the Koran respectively), writers such as al-Qirqisani wrote against such compromises. Argued al-Qirqisani,

> It would have been manifestly unjust of God to chastise children for sins committed during a previous existence, considering that the children neither have any recollection of these sins nor are able to grasp the meaning and cause of their suffering—whereas it is one of the cardinal earmarks of God's righteous punishment that the sufferer should be fully informed and conscious of the cause and justification of the chastisement meted out to him.[1]

We would also point out the problem of "infinite regress" in karmic theory. Infinite regress is where one has to continually "backpedal" to find the original cause for something. With the problem of evil and karmic reincarnation, one would have to keep "backpedaling" to find the original cause for evil:

$$\text{Evil} \longleftarrow \text{Cause}^1 \longleftarrow \text{Cause}^2 \longleftarrow \text{Cause}^3 \longleftarrow \text{etc.}$$

In other words:

Baby born with no arms		Previous life of hitting people		Previous life of being hot-tempered		etc.
	$\longleftarrow$		$\longleftarrow$		$\longleftarrow$	

But how does such an infinite regress to past lives solve the problem of the origin of evil? Under karmic circumstances, there is no origin of evil! How did suffering begin in the first place if each life of suffering is the result of a past life of sin? For reincarnationists claim that *any* life short of moral perfection entails suffering in order to help one along toward God.

Even if one tossed aside the idea of an infinite regress and just presumed a first life, there would be no karmic debt from a past life to explain all the evil and suffering one experienced during that first lifetime. "Thus the law of karma only postpones the solution to the problem of evil and suffering eternally, without ever confronting or solving the root of the dilemma."[2] In fact, Hick himself is doubtful of the validity of using reincarnation to solve the problem of evil. He admits that "it only pushes the problem back into earlier lives without thereby coming any nearer to a solution."[3]

An additional word should be said here about a Buddhist view of the no-self.[4] If you recall, Buddhism (see ch. 2) holds to the doctrine of anatta or "no-self." Those who interpret this doctrine as meaning that there is no continuity of the self after death—so that in effect, a different person is "reborn"—would seem to fall prey to a meaningless sense of karma. Unlike the Hindus, who believe that the same self is reincarnated in another body, the Buddhist view virtually obliterates the self.

The bottom line here is that once some doctrine of rebirth is affirmed, then it is either the same individual who is reborn or it is not. If it is the same individual who is reborn, then in what sense is that particular individual said to undergo a multiplicity of lives? Reincarnation inherently entails the notion that the same individual can be said to continue in another life without the continuation of the same body (not even in the same sex or life-form!). Thus, we seem to be left with only the memory and intellectual awareness of a person in order to meaningfully account for a continuation of the individual. But very few people claim to remember their "former lives," and even these few are doubtful (see ch. 4 and 5). Hence, if the individual cannot be identified through identity of body, memory, and/or intellectual awareness, then how can we make sense of the notion of a continuation of the individual in successive lives (reincarnation)?

If it is *not* the individual who is reborn, then why should someone pay for the karmic debt left by someone else? If this is what is meant by the doctrine of no-self, then it is not just.

For the one who is reborn finds herself in a situation that is outside of her control. For example, let's say that Martha has continually been kicking people all of her life. Then after Martha dies, she is reborn as Penny with a clubfoot (a different individual altogether). Penny now has a clubfoot for reasons *outside* of her control (i.e., in the control of Martha). But this is contrary to the justification for karma in the first place! For one of the "benefits" of believing in the doctrine of karma is that it supposedly solves the problem of evil by claiming that all of one's suffering is a result of past sins. Yet we now see that with the Buddhist doctrine of no-self, a person suffers as the result of *someone else's* sins.

The reincarnation "solution" to the problem of evil arises because of what is perceived to be weakness in classical Christian doctrines. We supposedly have no answer to the apparent difficulty in reconciling the existence of an omnipotent, loving God with the presence of suffering in the world. Our brief response to this objection is threefold.

First, Christians could answer the problem of evil by stating that some suffering of the innocent may be the result of something invaluably good, such as free will. It may be necessary for God to allow innocent suffering in order to give men full moral freedom. Second, *ultimate* justification for this suffering may be beyond this world. Evidence in this life may be lacking, but it is certainly possible that the suffering we observe will one day be seen as part of a larger plan for good and thus justified when the entire plan unfolds. Our finite minds may be unable to think of a good reason for what is apparently unjustifiable (let alone unjust), but this does not mean that an infinite being could not have some good reason. Third, evil may have a purpose in this world. For "few would deny the virtues of patience and mercy, yet patience cannot be produced without tribulation, nor mercy without tragedy."[5]

Finally, even Hick says that any amount of finite evil is justifiable in light of some future infinite good. Though we reject Hick's universalism, we accept his basic concept of the "infinite-future-good" defense. No matter how severe the suffering, in a finite world for a finite creature, the suffering will always be *finite*. And the promise and hope of *infinite* joy and bliss infinitely dwarf any amount of finite suffering.[6]

Whether the doctrines of reincarnation and karma involve the continuation of the self or not, they fail to provide an adequate solution to the problem of evil. In contrast, the Christian has solid, rational reasons for rejecting the doctrines of reincarnation and karma while, at the same time, offering a positive solution to the dilemma posed by the presence of evil.

KARMA AND THE LAW

Another way in which reincarnationists argue the validity of karma is by trying to demonstrate that it is a biblical belief. There is some truth to de Arteaga's plea for Christians to see karma in terms of a shadow truth containing elements that are biblically valid. Former professor of Old Testament in Heidelberg, Germany, Gerhard von Rad has examined what he calls the "act-consequence relationship" (which we will abbreviate as ACR) in the wisdom literature of the Old Testament. This principle simply states that certain consequences generally follow from certain acts.[7]

However, it would be an oversimplification to claim that the ACR, like karma, is a "doctrine of retribution." For unlike karma, the ACR in the Old Testament is not being subscribed to as a *universal law,* but as a *general principle* culled out "of experiences which had proved true for many generations."

ACR is a general principle of cause and effect, supporting the belief that good conduct brings about good results and evil conduct results in evil consequences (see Prov. 11:4, 28; 16:18). However, this principle is not to be considered an unbreakable absolute, contrary to the rigid doctrine of karma.

ACR is evidenced in the book of Job where Job's three friends attribute his sufferings to some previous sin(s) committed. Job recognized that his friends' standpoint had

> large elements of truth—retribution often does operate in the world. Its weakness is that it claims fully to explain the existence of evil, and from this inadequate premise it draws disastrous conclusions.[8]

Professor of Old Testament at Wycliffe College Roland K. Harrison in *Introduction to the Old Testament* notes that "one important aim of the book was to challenge the popular view that human suffering was self-entailed, and that justice was to be expected uniformly to occur in this life."

Harrison points out that the strong Hebrew belief in a personal, sovereign God, who ultimately is in control of all of life, kept the Hebrews from committing themselves to a karmic belief in a strictly enforced system of cause and effect. The relationship between cause and effect (sin and punishment) can be short-circuited by divine grace and forgiveness.

For example, God could allow the innocent to suffer in order to demonstrate his grandeur and purify the character of the sufferer (e.g., Job). God could also allow the wicked to prosper, thus demonstrating his grace and long-suffering (cf. Ps. 37:1ff.; 49:5ff.; 73:3ff.; Jer. 12:1ff.; Hab. 1:13ff.).

The law of karma is more in line with the faulty "uniform" view of retribution than with what von Rad has more insightfully labeled the "act-consequence relationship." In other words, for the Hebrew mind, an innocent and righteous individual like Job (1:8; 2:3) could suffer great evils without precipatory sins. When Job cried out to God, demanding that the Eternal Judge hear his case (Job 13:3, 14ff.; 23:3-5) and explain why he must suffer unjustifiably (9:34ff.; 10:2), God did not point to some past sin (much less a previous life).

Instead, God preached a sermon on his creation and preservation of the natural order, drawing the analogy that just as there are things concerning the physical sphere which Job could not understand, so there are things in the moral sphere which he could not fathom either. In short, Job must simply submit to the sovereign hand of God.

Furthermore, one should not draw a parallel between the Torah (Old Testament law) and karma. To do so would be to confuse categories. The Torah is a moral standard, it is the moral imperative. But karma is contentless. With respect to morality, it is really the *enforcement* of law rather than law itself.

The "reap what you sow"-type exhortations in Scripture (e.g., Gal. 6:7) fit into the category of some type of "enforcement" of the law (though it is not the law itself). However, as pointed out above, the general principle of "you reap what you sow" is von Rad's ACR, not karma's. It is generally true, not necessarily true. It can be transcended (i.e., by forgiveness); it is not "unbreakable" like karma.

Even the principle of determining just punishment in Exodus 21:26, 27 ("an eye for an eye") was not meant as a necessary and therefore "minimum" punitive law. Christopher Wright explains that "it was a limiting law, preventing excessive or vengeful punishment."[9] Hence, "this biblical injunction is not a mechanical law like karma, but is a conscious limitation placed upon the uncontrolled passions of human vengeance."[10]

KARMA IS ULTIMATELY
ANTI-HUMANITARIAN

Perhaps the most important and often noted Christian objection to the concept of karma is that karmic theologies tend to make persons passive towards social or personal evil and injustice.[11]

In *Reincarnation in Christianity* MacGregor admits that reincarnation in India "is inseparable from the cultural outlook. It is part of the mental furniture of the whole sub-continent." This is coupled by the fact that India has immense economic and social problems. The relationship between India's doctrine of karma and rebirth and its socio-economic problems can be seen as going hand in hand.

> India bears tragic witness to the problems associated with this thesis [of reincarnation]; despite all her poverty, starvation, suffering and chaos, India is the land where reincarnation has been taught the longest and most systematically.[12]

Kana Mitra, a native of India and adjunct professor of religion at LaSalle College and Villanova University, says that the hierarchical social order (i.e., caste system) of Hinduism is based on the differences among humans considered to be hereditary. Thus, being born in a particular caste is no accident but is dependent on one's actions in a previous life.

Gandhi himself disliked and tried to reject classifications of superiority and inferiority which were

> dependent on birth—yet he did not suggest any alternative for determination of caste. It seems that he, too, accepted uncritically the nonaccidental determination of birth by reincarnation and the law of karma. . . . It is evident that the establishment of human rights among Hindus demands not only social

reform movements, but also exploration, investigation, and reinterpretation of the theoretical foundations [e.g., the doctrines of reincarnation and karma] underlying the social hierarchy of Hinduism.[13]

Fatalism, lack of concern for the suffering of others, and general inaction are often traced to the two doctrines of reincarnation and karma. If one attempts to alleviate the burden of the sufferer, then the sufferer must endure greater hardship in the next life because she did not "pay off" her prescribed karmic debt. And ironically, this interference with karmic law would then constitute a "sin" and the would-be humanitarian would accumulate more karmic deposits. But if the reincarnationist does not interfere, that is, by not doing what he could do to prevent evil, *he* is doing an evil. Hence, reincarnationism becomes a source of what is evil, unjust, and inhumane.

EVOLUTION IS NOT TRUE OF EITHER THE PHYSICAL OR THE SPIRITUAL REALMS

Throughout reincarnationist writings is the assumption that our world came into being through a gradual process of evolution. Just as there is a gradual unfolding development in the physical world, so also is there a gradual development in the moral sphere. Notice that this argument from analogy *assumes* the reality of biological evolution.

Some overzealous evolutionists claim that evolution is a fact, not a theory. However, there are noted scientists who admit otherwise. G. A. Kerkut in his book *Implications of Evolution* acknowledges that evolution is nothing more than a "working hypothesis." Another evolutionist admitted that with the failure of these many efforts science was left in the somewhat embarrassing position of having to postulate theories of living origins which it could not demonstrate. After having chided the theologian for his reliance on myth and miracle, science found itself in the unenviable position of having to create a mythology of its own: namely, the assumption that what, after long effort, could not be proved to take place today had, in truth, taken place in the primeval past.[14]

In 1981, Colin Patterson, the head paleontologist of the British Museum, shocked the scientific community. Speaking to a group of top American scientists, he declared,

I think many people in this room would acknowledge that during the last few years, if you had thought about it at all, you have experienced a shift from evolution as knowledge to evolution as faith. . . . Evolution not only conveys no knowledge but seems somehow to convey antiknowledge.[15]

What is the reason for this honest pronouncement by an illustrious evolutionist? One reason is that after more than a hundred years of looking for Darwin's predicted missing links, not a single undisputed link has been found. Another reason is that after untold generations of experimentation with organisms (such as the fruit fly), scientists are unable to effect any significant permanent change. Only minor changes within species can be observed; no evolution between major types has been either observed in nature or produced in the laboratory. Physical evolution is a highly improbable theory for the origin of life and therefore, it serves as a brittle foundation for the doctrine of reincarnation.

PERFECTION NEED NOT BE GRADUAL

Unfortunately, despite the current scientific evidence against evolution, reincarnationists persist in using this model of gradual and progressive development in the moral and spiritual realm. Thus is opened Pandora's box of Eastern beliefs such as karma and a purgatorial reincarnation. MacGregor tells us, "On the reincarnationist view, one little life of whatever length . . . is not enough to weed out the garden of the soul. . . . The purificatory process takes a far longer time than we are likely to imagine."[16]

But the claim that we must have more than one lifetime for sufficient moral progress fails to consider the result of a comparison between finite humanity and an infinite God. Because the gap between a perfect God and imperfect human beings is so great, there will always be an *infinite* difference between the goodness of God and the goodness of man.

Moreover, even under the reincarnationists' own analogy of evolution, they admit that there can be quantum leaps of change. Why then cannot a quantum leap of moral evolution take place at death and/or at the resurrection of the saints?

Stephen Travis takes issue with Hick's presumption that we have no experience of instantaneous, radical change. Hick charges that such an immediate and radical change would destroy the continuity of the person so that after death he would not be the same person as before death. But "Hick himself argues that the life to come must be different from this life, beyond our powers to imagine." Why does Hick claim that a gradual purgatory-like state must exist (on the grounds that we have no experience of immediate, instantaneous transformation as moral beings) when his own scheme of the afterlife cannot escape some type of radical change as well?

Travis insightfully points out that

> the moment of conversion is a moment of fundamental
> and radical change which does not destroy the con-
> tinuity of the person. . . . It is no more difficult in
> principle to believe that at the moment of death or
> resurrection there takes place a moral transformation
> which is total and yet does not destroy the continuity
> of the person. By contrast, the argument for gradual
> purgation undermines the doctrine of God's grace.[17]

Travis's disagreement leads to another fundamental objection to "Christian" reincarnationism (which will be developed in the next chapter). In brief, Hick's claim that we
must pass through a series of stages toward ultimate fulfill-
ment presupposes an inadequate doctrine of grace.

SUMMARY

Travis's doctrines of reincarnation and karma do not fulfill
their claims to resolve the problem of evil or to parallel the
Old Testament law. Furthermore, they turn out to be ultimately anti-humanitarian, and therefore, anti-good. Their
analogies with evolution lie on tenuous ground since biological evolution cannot withstand criticism itself.

Finally, reincarnation falsely assumes the need for a slow,
earthly purgatory which ultimately contradicts the biblical
doctrine of grace. And since this Eastern dogma is anti-
grace, then it is also contrary to the biblical teaching of
salvation. Let us now focus our attention on this latter area.

CHAPTER 8
SALVATION AND REINCARNATION

Is God some divine schoolmaster of the cosmos who lovingly gives mankind more than just one lifetime to "pass the exam"? Human sentiment certainly sympathizes with such a notion at first glance. But is reincarnation really loving? Is it just?

In spite of our fundamental disagreement with the concept of universalism and the doctrine of "second" chance, the dislike of the doctrine of hell by reincarnationists expresses their sincere desire to give the unsaved every opportunity to "repent." Does the doctrine of salvation which flows out of the teachings of karma and reincarnation accord with Scripture and right reason?

KARMA IS INCOMPATIBLE WITH GRACE

The Christian doctrine of grace stands a great distance from the law of karma. For karma does not acknowledge the implications of the biblical notion of the atonement. The atonement refers to the act by which God and humanity are reconciled.

The biblical view of the atonement is comprised of what

is called the "penal satisfaction" of God's wrath. In other words, because of God's absolute holiness, he must judge sin. If sin were to be just swept aside, then God would not be truly just and holy.

Yet out of his mercy, God provided a way of escaping sin's penalty—God's wrath. His wrath was poured out on Someone else—Someone so morally innocent and pure that he could justly pay for our sins. The Scriptures teach that the atonement which Christ procured for us should be understood as a penal satisfaction (i.e., it satisfied the demands of God's absolute holiness). And since the atonement is understood as penal satisfaction, then there is no need to pay off one's karmic debt in some future life. If the death of Christ totally satisfied the punitive demands of the righteous law of God, then what need is there for more payment?

Christ "satisfied" the debt of sin owed to God.[1] *Hilaskomai*, which means "to placate; appease" (Rom. 3:25; Heb. 2:17; 1 John 2:2; 4:10), is the word used in the New Testament to convey this idea of "satisfaction." But the New Testament evidence of a penal satisfaction theory of the atonement rests on more than a single word.

The New Testament concepts and metaphors of Jesus argue for his work of atonement being one of "satisfaction." Jesus is depicted as:

- A ransom for us (Matt. 20:28);
- The sin-bearer (2 Cor. 5:21; Heb. 7:26, 27; 1 Pet. 2:24);
- The Suffering Servant (Acts 3:13; 8:32ff.; cf. Isa. 42, 49, 50, 53);
- The Redeemer whose purchase is made with blood (Acts 20:28);
- The curse-bearer (Gal. 3:13; cf. Deut. 21:22ff.); and
- The Lamb of sacrifice (John 1:29, 36; Acts 8:32; 1 Pet. 1:19).

The atonement is seen as a sacrifice, a substitution, reconciliation, redemption, and justification. These major descriptions of the atonement or its effectual results also argue for a satisfaction theory of the atonement:

- Sacrifice has as it primary purpose, propitiation.
- Substitution: Christ substituted his holy life for our sinful ones, thereby appeasing the wrath of God, who cannot tolerate sin.
- Reconciliation is the putting at an end the enmity between God and man. And since this "enmity" is sin, which incurs the wrath of God, the act of reconciliation must have satisfied this divine wrath.
- Redemption assumes a price which was paid for a ransom. When related to the work of Christ, this price was the life of Christ himself (Mark 10:45), which satisfied the debt owed.
- Justification: if the penalty for sin is the wrath of God against sin, and justification is the acquittal of humankind's sin, then the atonement is the just satisfaction of God's wrath.

Theologian William G. T. Shedd makes a distinction between "personal" and "vicarious" atonement. His distinction demonstrates the difference between the biblical picture of atonement (vicarious) and the one espoused by reincarnationists (personal atonement).

ATONEMENT

Personal	Vicarious
Made by the offending party	Made by the party offended
Given by the criminal	Received by the criminal
Incompatible with mercy	Highest form of mercy

Hence, Shedd notes that

> when the sinner satisfies the law by his own eternal death, he experiences justice without mercy; but when God satisfies the law for him, he experiences mercy in the wonderful form of God's self-sacrifice. . . . Vicariousness implies *substitution*. A vicar is a person deputed to perform the function of another.[2]

The New Testament teaching is uniformly one which affirms that it is God who propitiates, appeases, satisfies, and reconciles. None of these are the acts of the creature. God himself is the originating and active agent. Thus as Robert Morey aptly puts it,

> Christianity eventually displaced Karmic transmigration with its doctrine of Christ's substitutionary atonement in which He paid all of our "Karmic debt" through His own suffering. He had no Karma of His own, but He suffered and died for our sins.[3]

The reincarnationist's objection to this concept of the atonement is that one's karmic debt must be paid by the self because it would be immoral for someone else to pay for it. Admittedly, the doctrine of substitutionary atonement has two moral principles in a real conflict:

- Principle 1: The innocent should not be punished for sins he never committed (Ezek. 18:20);
- Principle 2: One should do his best to save others even to the point of self-sacrifice (Mark 10:45; Luke 19:10; John 15:13).

Christ was innocent, and yet he willingly allowed himself to be punished for our sins (Isa. 53; 1 Pet. 2:24; 3:18; 2 Cor. 5:21). He was "squeezed between the demands of justice for the innocent (Himself) and love for the guilty (mankind)."[4]

Time and space do not allow for a detailed discussion. However, it will be noted here that we accept what has been termed the "hierarchical ethic." Briefly, "hierarchicalism" says that, in the face of unavoidable conflicts between moral absolutes, "God does not hold a person guilty for not keeping a lower moral law so long as he keeps the higher. That is, God exempts one from his duty to keep the lower law since he could not keep it without breaking a higher law."[5]

In other words, there is a hierarchy of moral commands which we are to follow within their respective priorities. For example, we are commanded in Scripture to obey both God, and human government (see Rom. 13:1ff.). Yet at times obeying human government conflicts with obeying God. In those cases, we should obey God's higher moral law, which exempts us from keeping the lower law of human government. In fact, this is exactly what Peter and John did when they refused to obey the commands of the human authorities to stop preaching (Acts 4:1-31). Likewise, when a soldier falls on an enemy hand grenade to diffuse its impact on his platoon, he is not guilty of suicide but is to be praised for his sacrificial love.

Thus, our answer with respect to the atonement is that Christ was not immoral when he overrode the need to defend the innocent (himself) by his concern for the salvation of the guilty (mankind). Even if reincarnationists find this view unacceptable, they must admit that it is a logical possibility in keeping with the traditional view of the atonement. Christ chose to suspend the lower moral mandate, which says that we should not commit suicide, in order to fulfill the higher moral law of saving the lives of others.

While some so-called "Christian" forms of reincarnation

are said to be compatible with forgiveness, the same cannot be said for their *non*-Christian counterparts. In his book *Reincarnation: The Cycle of Necessity* Manly Hall curtly remarks, "The belief in the doctrine of the forgiveness of sin is entirely inconsistent with a recognition of the immutability of universal law." He notes the frequent efforts to blend the doctrine of vicarious atonement with that of reincarnation and karma. We agree with Hall on the point that when reincarnationists have tried to mix grace with karma, the result is

> hopeless confusion and contradiction. Laws were not laws. There were unexplainable exceptions which plagued the mind as irregular verbs plague the schoolboy. . . . The consequence was a distorted Christian theology ornamented with Eastern terms and some comparatively inconsequential Eastern dogma. Exceptions destroyed the rule.[6]

Karma is incompatible with grace because fundamentally it is a salvation by works. MacGregor states his case clearly:

> What, according to the mainstream of orthodox Christian teaching, does Christ do for us? What is the nature of his redemptive work? However the various theological traditions express it, it is always seen as a provision of the conditions that make possible my salvation. Through faith in him I am justified, that is, I am "put in the right way," so that it is now possible for me, as it was not before, to get myself out of the mess I was in and be "sanctified." We might express that by saying that whereas I had got into such a bind that, practically speaking, my moral evolution had come to

a halt and further progress was impossible, Christ has come to my aid in such a way that by appropriating his spiritual power I can make my progress once again.[7]

Moreover, Howe finds it appalling that *grace* salvation, "stated in its most extreme form, . . . concedes no merit to man and all merit to God, who will finally uplift his undeserving creature."[8] MacGregor gives himself away when he confesses, "Those of us who are of an individualistic turn of mind are likely to find reincarnationism an exciting concept if only because it so conspicuously exalts the individual."[9]

Hence, according to reincarnationism, the atonement did not provide for my being declared righteous; it merely afforded the *conditions* which made my moral progress possible. We respond by saying that true moral evolution, or growth, is not so much a *process* as it is a *choice*—a choice to accept Jesus Christ as our Savior by grace alone (Eph. 2:8, 9), and then to love our fellowman and do what is morally right.

Virtually everything written on the subject of reincarnation speaks of salvation by works: one can pay off one's "karmic debt," thereby securing a better position in the next life, by working hard in this life. Salvation (if one may call it that) is a reward for one's own efforts. It might be said that the notion of salvation by works is even more fundamental to popular reincarnation theory than the doctrine of successive lives: these lives are just the necessary fields in which the labor can be accomplished. . . . The number of our earthly lives is irrelevant to salvation, since God is completely unimpressed by our attempts to pay off a debt that He alone could and did pay on the cross of Jesus Christ.[10]

"Christian" reincarnationist Hearney has said, "I believe that if one presents a doctrine of karma bereft of grace, then reincarnation is totally incompatible with the God of Christianity."[11] And as we have shown earlier, the only kind of law of karma that is meaningful is indeed "bereft of grace."

KARMA IS ULTIMATELY IMPERSONAL

"Christian" reincarnationists would like to make the law of karma and Christianity compatible. This seems inherently inconsistent since the Christian view of judgment is one which contains ultimate justice, delivered by a *personal* God who can forgive, justify, and free us from our karmic debt. In contrast, karma is *mechanical*. It is "automatic," "inexorable," and "unalterable," according to MacGregor.

Either karma can be overridden or it cannot. If karma is "unbreakable," then how does it allow for forgiveness? On the other hand, if it is "breakable," then past evil deeds can be forgiven, the sinner can be declared righteous, and there is no need for future incarnations.

MacGregor and others would like to think that the Lord and/or the individual chooses his own destiny. The law of karma is supposedly not impersonal in the sense that it was *my* past actions which brought about my present circumstances. But the question arises: Can I or the Lord choose my next incarnation contrary to the law of karma? Must I suffer or "pay" for my past evil deeds? Or, can my sins be wiped away as if never committed in a grand and sweeping act of forgiveness? If so, then there is no need for reincarnational karma. If not, then karma* is mechanically conceived.

De Arteaga notes that "at best, the concept of karma reduces God to a distant, impersonal force." This is a radical departure from "the Jewish and Christian traditions, where, since the Psalms of David, God's mercy and forgiveness have been revealed as fundamental to the character of God's being and activity."[12] Thus, the doctrine of karma can in no way be reconciled with the God of the Bible.

HELL AND THE LOVE OF GOD

From scholars to pop enthusiasts, believers in reincarnation share a common abhorrence of the doctrine of hell. "Christian" reincarnationists seek to prove that reincarnationism fits better with the idea of a loving God than does the biblical doctrine of hell. Without the concept of an ultimate judgment (hell), only intermediate judgments (reincarnational purgatories) are necessary. However, as the following discussion demonstrates, ultimate justice (hell) is indeed compatible with the existence of a loving God.

The love of God cannot be understood apart from his justice and holiness. The demands of love, especially divine love, are intertwined with a deeply moral sensibility. Jesus said, "If you love Me, you will keep My commandments" (John 14:15). And again, "He who has My commandments and keeps them, he it is who loves Me" (John 14:21). In fact, Jesus himself manifested perfect love as he obediently subjected himself to the cross as the heavenly Father willed (Luke 22:42; John 10:17; Heb. 10:9).

It is therefore too simplistic to brush aside the doctrine

---

*To say that karma is "breakable" should not be confused with affirming that the law is relative. On the contrary, moral law is absolute. However, karma technically does not refer to the moral law itself; it only refers to the *enforcement* of the law (see ch. 7).

of everlasting punishment by invoking the divine attribute of love. Morey in *Death and the Afterlife* rightly states that we should not try "to base man's salvation solely upon God's attributes, such as His love or goodness." Scripture combines God's love for the world together with the sacrificial atonement of his Son (John 3:16; Rom. 5:8). God's holiness is so great that he cannot simply forget about our sins. And yet, God's love is so vast that he provided the means by which our sins can be forgiven.

This is tough love, a holy love; not a sentimental love which arbitrarily disregards justice.

> Thus God's love, in and of itself, cannot save anyone, much less all of humanity. None of God's attributes, in and of themselves, can save anyone. It is the manifestation of God's love in Christ that saves sinners, not "love" as mere sentiment.[13]

And since a holy requirement (Christ's death for our sins) is necessary for entrance into heaven, it would naturally follow that those who do not appropriate his vicarious atonement will not enter heaven. Hell is not a rare doctrine in the Bible. Indeed, Jesus himself taught extensively on the doctrine of eternal punishment (Matt. 8:12; 13:42; 25:30, 41, 46; Mark 9:43-48; Luke 16:19-31).

REINCARNATIONISTS' DOCTRINE OF HELL
The biblical teaching of "hell" is simply a hypothetical threat to help people receive the gospel. As presented in chapter six, Hick stated that the following two biblical ideas do not contradict each other:

- Unless you repent you will surely perish.
- In the end all will turn from their wickedness and live.[14]

While we must admit that these two statements do not contradict each other, Christian philosopher Paul Helm criticizes the value and meaningfulness of such a combination. For Hick is proposing to make compatible two opposing beliefs:

- The real threat of hell
- Hell does not exist

Helm contends that such a proposal reduces to one of two positions.

- "Soft" universalism: the threats could be ignored but will not be.
- "Hard" universalism: God "structures" human nature in such a way that all men will finally be saved.[15]

As a soft universalist, Hick would see no problem with the moral character of Jesus if Jesus posed a threat that would not be carried out. However, if Jesus did not really intend to threaten, but merely gave the impression that he was threatening, then this would make Jesus guilty of intentionally misleading his hearers. On the other hand, if Jesus truly intended to threaten his hearers with hell in order to save them, then such a threat must be real. That is, there must be some meaningful content to a threat in order for it to be bonafide. "A threat that the threatener is unwilling to carry out is hollow and not a threat."[16] Hick's soft universalism makes our Lord's threats about as forceful as trying to sink a battleship with a peashooter. Shedd says that

to threaten with "everlasting punishment" a class of persons described as "goats upon the left hand" of the Eternal Judge, while knowing at the same time that this class would ultimately have the same holiness and happiness with those described as "sheep upon the right hand" of the Judge, would have been both falsehood and folly. The threatening would have been false.[17]

Helm concludes that soft universalism fares no better than the traditional doctrine of eternal punishment. Paradoxically, the soft universalist wants to preserve God's goodness by denying that Jesus really taught about a real hell. And yet, is God's goodness preserved when he threatens people with an unreal hell? "What is the difference, so far as the character of the threatener is concerned, between a successful and an unsuccessful threat?" If God's moral character remains undimished by the fact that he *allows* persons to freely choose evil, then this holds true when some actually *choose* evil and go to hell in accordance with his threats.

Taken as a "hard" universalist, Hick would be proposing that it is not possible for anyone to be unsaved. But if it is impossible for anyone to be lost, then Jesus did not offer any genuine threats. As we noted earlier, there must be the possibility of an action being carried out in order for a threat to be genuinely *threatening*. Helm argues two things:[18]

- Soft universalism offers no moral superiority to the traditional doctrine of eternal punishment.
- Hard universalism reduces Jesus' language to no threat at all, which poses a real difficulty not only for Hick's proposal, but for the moral integrity of Jesus himself.

Not only can Hick's universalism be shown to be meaningless, but on the positive side, we can demonstrate how the doctrine of eternal punishment is compatible with an all-good, all-loving God. In regard to eternal punishment, Shedd said,

> Nothing is requisite for its maintenance but the admission of three cardinal truths of theism [the Christian worldview]: namely, that there is a just God; that man has a free will; and that sin is voluntary action.[19]

G. K. Chesterton is said to have gone as far as to say, "Hell is the greatest compliment God has ever paid to the dignity of human freedom."[20]

In short, we can intelligently argue that universalism is wrong and ultimate judgment is right because God allows us to respond freely to his love. If a person does not want to be loved, God does not force his will upon him. Thus God in essence is saying to us all, " 'Be it as you wish, forever.' Heaven and hell, then, are merely a permanentizing of what men freely will."[21]

Understood in this light, universalism turns out to be an argument for the anti-benevolence of God. And conversely, the doctrine of ultimate judgment argues for the love of God and the dignity of man.

However, Hick contends that universalism is compatible with free will because the free will defense has a "vulnerable premise": "that God can only ensure that all men will eventually be saved if he is prepared if necessary to coerce some of them, however subtly."[22] To put it another way, in Hick's view, we weakly argue that the only way God can save all humanity is to forcibly drag them into the kingdom.

But while Hick does not make God force man into the kingdom *externally*, he does make God force man *internally*. He words this very carefully by saying that God made us to be "inwardly structured towards" himself. That is,

God created us in such a way that we would respond to him because of some inherent trait he placed in our nature. Hence, Hick says that "the notion of divine coercion is set aside by the fact of divine creation." But isn't this simply a divine "stacking of the deck"?[23] With Hick, coercion is "built-in." His tact does not negate the traditional argument against universalism.

Hell should be understood "figuratively" as annihilation. We may now return to the second option open to the reincarnationist who rejects the concept of hell. MacGregor concedes that universalism may not be possible in light of free will.

> If, however, one were to return thousands of times, begin all over again, perhaps even in another galaxy, and still fail to grow in any direction no matter what kind of soil or sunshine or rain might be provided for one's growth, surely nothing in the economy of the cosmos could be served by the continuation of the futile process.[24]

Rejecting the "barbarous" notion of everlasting punishment, MacGregor writes,

> The notion that many people might be simply extinguished, fading gradually out of existence, seems to me more intelligible. Such people do not want existence. Why, then, should the gift be thrust upon them?[25]

But who says that these people do not "want" existence? Even the famous atheist Friedrich Nietzsche in his book *The Genealogy of Morals* implied that he would rather choose eternally conscious suffering (i.e., hell) than to cease to exist.

MacGregor may have to face the fact that while a person may not *want* to be in hell, she may *will* it. And if then MacGregor should adjust his doctrine of annihilation by claiming that such a person can justifiably be "snuffed" out of existence because she did not *choose* to exist (e.g., by rejecting Christ), would this not be the identical argument used by those who hold to the traditional doctrine of hell? Do we not also argue that some are justifiably separated from God eternally (i.e., hell) because they do not choose to be forever with him (i.e., heaven)?

We could also question the justice of a God who would simply "snuff" out of existence those who did not choose his way. MacGregor's theory would also neglect passages which affirm the resurrection of the wicked (John 5:28, 29; Acts 24:15; Dan. 12:2).

Another complaint hurled by reincarnation advocates is that the doctrine of hell is the height of penal overkill, for no amount of finite sin, however great, could deserve infinite punishment. Clearly, the crucial premise here is the assumption that the rejection of Christ is a "finite debt." But there are several reasons why this sin is not finite in nature. First:

> The endlessness of future punishment, . . . is implied in the endlessness of guilt and condemnation. . . . All suffering in the next life, therefore, of which the sufficient and justifying reason is guilt, must continue as long as the reason continues; and the reason is everlasting. . . . The *continuous* nature of guilt necessitates the endlessness of retribution.[26]

Shedd thus defends the rationality of endless punishment from the nature of sin. The rejection of Christ is a qualitatively infinite sin since it is committed against an infinite God.

Second, the fact that one of the persons of the Godhead was incarnated, taking on human flesh and then sacrificing himself on our behalf, "demonstrates the infinity of the evil." For Shedd finds it incredible that the Eternal God should have submitted to such a tremendous self-sacrifice, to remove a finite and temporal evil.

Third, just because sin is committed in finite time does not make it a finite evil, deserving of merely finite suffering. Just because it only took a few minutes to reject Christ does not make it a few minutes worth of sin. Punishment for a crime is not determined by the time that was taken to commit it.

> But even in human punishment, no reference is had to the length of the time occupied in the commission of the offense. Murder is committed in an instant, and theft sometimes requires hours. But the former is the greater crime, and receives the greater punishment.[27]

The gravity of the sin is determined by its object (the infinitely holy God). Therefore, sin against the Eternal is worthy of unending punishment.

Fourth, it could be argued that even the everlasting suffering of a finite being does not completely satisfy the just demands of an infinite crime. For any amount of suffering endured by a finite and limited being will be just that, finite and limited. Any crime against God is infinite, and thus requires infinite punishment. But no finite being could serve such a sentence! There is, therefore, no over-punishment in endless punishment.

To close this section on the compatibility between hell and a loving God, it is interesting to note that even Nicolas

Berdiaev (a universalist), who finds the doctrine of eternal punishment "devilish," "hideous and morally revolting," admits that

> the doctrine of reincarnation, which has obvious advantages, involves, however, another nightmare—the nightmare of endless incarnation, of infinite wanderings along dark passages; it finds the solution of man's destiny in the cosmos and not in God.[28]

ONE LIFETIME IS ENOUGH

In line with the preceding objection, reincarnationists demand that we have more than one opportunity to be saved because one life is too short for adequate moral progress. Such is the reasoning of reincarnationists who parallel reincarnation with purgatory. But throughout John Wenham's critical examination of Scripture entitled *The Goodness of God,* he found that

> the Bible nowhere teaches the existence of a place for slow purgation after death. On the contrary it teaches that at the end of the age, at Christ's second coming, there will be immediate and instantaneous change for those who are in union with Christ, so that they become like him, whereas those who do not belong to Christ will have to face their judgment in their sins.[29]

However, it should be noted here that Wenham also believes in annihilation as the judgment for unbelievers.

John Snyder offers a weighty argument against this more-than-one-time opportunity theory in his book *Reincarnation vs. Resurrection.* The reincarnationist assumes that somehow it makes good sense to compare thousands of years or more with eternity, but not seventy years. Whether one compares seventy years or seventy thousand years with infinity, the time will always be infinitesimally small compared to unending existence.[30]

Once again, we discover, under careful scrutiny, that the reincarnationist argument is subject to the same criticism it raises against its traditional counterpart.

In addition, reincarnationists fail to find fault with the traditional argument that a lifetime is long enough to make a lifetime decision. MacGregor's analogy of the compassionate teacher who gives his student another chance to resit an exam is inappropriate and arbitrary. We could just as profoundly (even more so) suggest the analogy of shooting oneself in the head. There is little chance of a second opportunity in this illustration. Not all trials in life afford limitless nor even multiple opportunities.

Hebrews 9:27 also argues against the doctrine of a "second chance": "It is appointed for men to die once and after this comes judgment." The original Greek word for "appointed" *(apokeimai)* is in the present tense, indicating that this is continually true. Also, the tense of "to die" *(apotaneiv)* affirms that death is a conclusive act. In *The Hindu View of Life* Neo-Hindu apologist S. Radhakrishnan admits this verse points out the essential difference between Christian and Hindu thought.

And if reincarnationists try to escape this meaning by claiming that this death refers to only *spiritual* death rather than *physical* death, then in context Christ's sacrificial crucifixion would only entail a spiritual death as well. But this is clearly wrong for the Bible teaches that Christ died physically: He "tasted death" (Heb. 2:9). He was "offered once to bear the sins of many" (Heb. 9:28). In fact, the whole section of Hebrews 8-10 rests upon the very real physical death of our crucified Lord.

SUMMARY

The doctrines of karma and reincarnation do not solve the problem of evil (ch. 7), nor do they make rational or biblical sense in regard to personal salvation. The so-called evidences for reincarnation from the areas of psychology (ch. 4-5) and justice (ch. 6-8) fall far short of their intended goal. We now turn to the final major area of "evidence" used by reincarnationists—the Bible.

CHAPTER 9
THE BIBLE AND REINCARNATION

Reincarnationists, whether claiming to be Christians or not, often turn to the Scriptures for proof and/or confirmation of their doctrine of rebirth. Many "Christian" reincarnationists admit that reincarnation is not expressly taught in Scripture, but MacGregor has noted that "neither is the doctrine of the Trinity." The ambiguity of one's life after death is much like the equally mysterious character of God's trinitarian nature.

Any argument concerning reincarnation in the biblical text is seriously hampered by the fact that there is very little in the New Testament pertaining to the prenatal and postmortem life of man. Therefore, we should not ask such questions as "Does the New Testament teach reincarnation or not? If it does, where is the text? If it does not, how dare we encourage a plainly unbiblical doctrine?" For this would be

> a radically wrong approach. If we were to use it we would obscure truth rather than display it. We must try to see, rather, whether reincarnation is or is not the sort of doctrine that would have been in the minds

of the biblical writers and then see, so far as we can, what sort of attitude they would have taken towards it. In short, their witness need not be expressed in a specific text.[1]

The question for the so-called "Christian" reincarnationist is whether or not the Scriptures *allow* for a reincarnational scheme of the afterlife. The following are passages most commonly used by those who deem the doctrine of reincarnation worthy of the company of Christianity.

JOB 1:20, 21

Then Job arose and tore his robe and shaved his head, and he fell to the ground and worshiped. And he said, *"Naked I came from my mother's womb, and naked I shall return there.* The Lord gave and the Lord has taken away. Blessed be the name of the Lord" (emphasis added).

Does this poetic phrase refer to reincarnation? Actually scholars have found that the Hebrew word for "womb" *(shammah)* is used here in a figurative sense to depict the "earth" from which we came. This alludes to Genesis 3:19 where God curses Adam with physical death:

Till you return to the ground, because from it you were taken; for you are dust, and to dust you shall return.

The ideas of "earth" and "womb" are put together in Psalm 139: 13, 15:

For Thou didst form my inward parts; Thou didst weave me in my mother's womb. . . . My frame was not hidden from Thee, when I was made in secret, and skillfully wrought in the depths of the earth.

This is borne out in Ecclesiasticus 40:1 by the ancient Hebrew writer Ben Sira:

Much labor was created for every man, and a heavy yoke is upon the sons of Adam, from the day they come forth from their mother's womb, till the day they return to the Mother of all.

JEREMIAH 1:4, 5; GALATIANS 1:15, 16

Now the word of the Lord came to me saying, "Before I formed you in the womb I knew you, and before you were born I consecrated you; I have appointed you a prophet to the nations" (Jer. 1:4, 5).

But when He who had set me apart, even from my mother's womb, and called me through His grace, was pleased to reveal His Son in me, that I might preach Him among the Gentiles . . . (Gal. 1:15, 16).

These passages are sometimes used to show that they refer to a pre-existent state of the individual, i.e., Jeremiah and Paul. During this alleged preexistent state, Jeremiah and Paul were appointed for their respective ministries. But the phrase "I knew you" does not refer to God having some kind of intellectual relationship with a preexistent Jeremiah. Rather, it refers to their prenatal existence in their mother's womb where they were a person from the moment of conception (Pss. 51:7; 139:13-16).

The Hebrew word used here for "to know" *(yada)* goes "beyond mere intellectual knowledge to personal commitment."[2] It was used in the political arena to describe the commitment of a vassal (servant) to his lord. For example, in Amos 3:2 this word is used as a description of the relationship between Israel and the Lord God: "You only have I chosen [*yada*] among all the families of the earth; therefore, I will punish you for all your iniquities."

This commitment-oriented use of "to know" *(yada)* is supported by the other verbs used to describe God's relationship with Jeremiah: "consecrated" and "appointed" are words pointing to a specific assignment that God had for Jeremiah (cf. Gen. 1:17; 17:5; Ex. 7:1; Isa. 49:6). Therefore, the passage in Jeremiah does not suggest preexistence; it denotes God's special purpose for Jeremiah as a prophet, even in his mother's womb.

Likewise, the Galatians passage does the same thing with Paul. The terms used in this passage are the same as those used in Romans 1:1: "Paul, a bond-servant of Christ Jesus, called as an apostle, set apart for the gospel of God." Paul was "set apart" before his birth in the sense that he was set apart for a mission—to spread the good news of Jesus Christ among the Gentiles.

MATTHEW 11:14; 17:10-13; MARK 9:11-13; LUKE 1:17

And if you care to accept it, he himself is Elijah, who was to come (Matt. 11:14).

And His disciples asked Him, saying, "Why then do the scribes say that Elijah must come first?" And He answered and said, "Elijah is coming and will restore all things; but I say to you, that Elijah already came, and they did not recognize him, but did to him whatever they wished. So also the Son of Man is going to suffer at their hands." Then the disciples understood that He had spoken to them about John the Baptist (Matt. 17:10-13; see also Mark 9:11-13).

"And it is he who will go as a forerunner before Him in the spirit and power of Elijah, to turn the hearts of the fathers back to the children, and the disobedient to the attitude of the righteous; so as to make ready a people prepared for the Lord" (Luke 1:17).

In these passages, Jesus affirmed the fact that in order for the Messiah to be present at that time, Elijah had to have come first (Mal. 4:5). Jesus also affirmed that Elijah had in fact "already come" in the person of John the Baptist. This leads "Christian" reincarnationists to conclude that John the Baptist was therefore a reincarnation of Elijah.

The phrase in Luke's description of John the Baptist, "in the spirit and power of Elijah," does not bother de Arteaga. He concludes that "Lucan scripture could mean 'besides John the Baptist being Elijah, he has reappeared with his spirit and power.' "[3] Furthermore, Luke does not "depersonalize" the Elijah-John the Baptist relationship by the use of "spirit" since the New Testament usage of spirit often refers to personality (e.g., 1 Cor. 5:5). Howe also argues that in order "for the messianic prophecy of Malachi to be fully realized, John the Baptist must *be* Elijah."[4]

De Arteaga points out another reason for understanding these passages as probable evidence for reincarnation. He says that "the most serious difficulty in 'watering down' Jesus' equivalency description of the [Elijah-John the Baptist relationship] is that Jesus used equivalency statements *only when he meant them.*" For example, in John 10:30, Jesus says, "I and the Father are one." De Arteaga's reasoning here is that if the identity between Elijah and John the Baptist is diluted, then so must the relationship be between Jesus and the Father God (cf. John 6:46-49).

Howe bases his line of reasoning on contemporary biblical scholarship, claiming that "a plausible case can be made that Jesus and John the Baptist accepted reincarnation, having learned of it through the Essenes." The Essenes were a secretive, monastic brotherhood of Jews that flourished in Palestine from the second century B.C. to the second century A.D. Howe does admit that whether or not the Essenes specifically believed in reincarnation cannot be proven. His claim that the Essenes did in fact believe in reincarnation is founded upon the following evidences cited by the Jewish historian Josephus:

- The Essenes lived in accord with the regulations of the Greek philosopher Pythagoras, who in turn is associated in antiquity with the doctrine of reincarnation.
- The Essenes held to two "fundamental" tenets of reincarnation; preexistence and the divinity of the soul.[5]

And yet, while there may be a parallel between the messianic expectations of the Essenes and those fulfilled by Jesus, the link between Jesus and the Essene sect is admittedly suspect since the Essene characteristics of asceticism, legalism, and secrecy are absent in the teachings of Jesus. Howe, therefore, looks for a contact between Jesus and the Essenes through Jesus' relationship with John the Baptist. He believes John's lifestyle (Matt. 3:4), fast-growing ministry (Matt. 3:5), and emphasis on the cleansing waters of baptism are proof enough that John was associated with the Essenes.

Jesus was baptized by John and "he even states explicitly that he was the disciple of John (Matt. 11:11)." Rather than the "mistranslated" version of "He who is least in the kingdom of heaven is greater than he," the more defensible translation is

"He who is less [Jesus, the disciple] is greater than he [John the Baptist] in the kingdom of heaven." Seen in this light, the passage would be a claim on the part of Jesus that although he had at one time been less than John in the here and now, he is greater in the kingdom of heaven.[6]

Howe also argues that recently it has been pointed out that the word "younger" or "lesser" was the rabbinic term for a "disciple." Moreover, the "conventional" rendering would exclude John from the kingdom of heaven. Perhaps Howe says this because he understands the phrase "least in the kingdom of heaven" to refer to those who *barely* qualified for kingdom membership.

Armed with these interpretations, Howe deduces that if the Essenes believed in reincarnation and Jesus was a disciple of John the Baptist, whom he alleges to be an Essene, it follows that Jesus held to the doctrine of reincarnation. And while Howe confesses that the Dead Sea Scroll findings are contrary to Josephus's report of the Essenes, he still asserts that "for one who wishes to establish a direct connection between Jesus and the doctrine of reincarnation, here is a defensible argument based upon the working assumptions of recent New Testament scholarship."[7]

All of these arguments fail to establish that John the Baptist was the reincarnation of Elijah. For one thing, Elijah could not have reincarnated as John—at least in terms of standard reincarnationism—because Elijah never died (2 Kings 2:11; cf. Heb. 11:5). Josephus himself noted that at the time of Jesus the Jews believed that Elijah had been hidden by God until he could descend back again.[8]

The appearance of Elijah on the Mount of Transfiguration, not as John the Baptist (his supposedly last reincarnation) but as his "former" self, also argues against the probability of a reincarnation.

Whether or not one takes John as the reincarnation of

Elijah, there would seem to be an apparent conflict between Jesus' affirmation of John as the Elijah that "already came" (Matt. 17:11-13) and John's denial of it (John 1:21). Bible scholars, however, do not find Jesus' affirmation and John's denial to be contradictory. There was a sense in which John was Elijah in that he fulfilled the ministry that Malachi had foretold (cf. Mal. 4:5; Isa. 40:3; Luke 1:17). But the Jews remembered Elijah as one who escaped death and left the earth in a chariot of fire (2 Kings 2:11). If they expected this identical, ascended Elijah to reappear, then John was certainly not Elijah. Walter Kaiser states,

> Even when it is clear that John only denied being Elijah in the popular misconceptions entertained by the people of John's day, John could be identified as Elijah only because the same spiritual power that had energized Elijah had now fallen on him.[9]

Luke 1:17 makes more specific this aspect of similarity without identity. John was a forerunner of Christ *"in the spirit and power of Elijah."* The meaning of this verse is clearly seen from the story of Elijah in 2 Kings 2:9-18. Before Elijah's earthly departure, his disciple Elisha wished to "inherit a double portion" of Elijah's "spirit." After the whirlwind had taken Elijah up, Elisha parted the waters of the Jordan with his master's mantle and crossed over to Jericho. When "the sons of the prophet" saw Elisha, they said, "The spirit of Elijah rests on Elisha."

Obviously this does not mean that Elisha was a reincarnation of Elijah since they were both alive at the same time. It means that he continued the prophetic ministry with the same spirit and power of Elijah in fulfilling the duties (Elijah's) and the prophecy regarding him. Therefore, the most that can be inferred from this passage is that the role of Elijah was filled in a functional way by John the Baptist.

Oscar Cullman in his book *The Christology of the New Testament* points out that the Hebrews thought in terms of function, while the Greeks thought more in terms of nature. So, from a Greek's perspective, the affirmation— "John the Baptist *was* Elijah"—would infer that they were the same *being,* whereas the Hebrew mindset could very well have been thinking of an equivalency in function (cf. Matt. 17:10-13; Mark 9:11-13).

In response to Howe's argument that Jesus probably believed in reincarnation as a result of his acquaintance with the "Essene" John the Baptist, we offer the following evidence. Howe admits that Jesus could not have been an Essene; and yet he tries to connect Jesus with the Essenes through his relationship with John the Baptist. Notice that even *if* John were an Essene, Howe's own reasoning is inconsistent. For if Jesus did not learn the Essene beliefs in "asceticism, legalism, and secrecy" through his "discipleship" under John the Baptist, why should we suppose that Jesus learned the alleged Essene belief in reincarnation?

In any case, while it is helpful to recognize the similarities between John and the Essenes, we should also recognize his uniqueness. The following is a summary of the evidence presented by F. F. Bruce in his work, *New Testament History*.[10] John was unique and different from the Essenes in a number of ways:

- He was a "wonder-child," born by special intervention of the Holy Spirit (Luke 1:80).
- He was distinctively prophetic (Luke 3:2).
- His audience was public not private and isolated.
- His baptism was distinctive on two counts: it was administered to others (Essene baptism was performed by

the self and for the self) and had a future significance (looked toward the coming kingdom of God).

Thus, even if John was influenced by an Essene group, which has yet to be proven by modern scholarship, he was unique in his ministry and function. Hence, even *if* the Essenes held to reincarnation, and *if* John was at some time connected with the Essenes, there is still no need (nor even probably reason) to think that John believed in reincarnation, thereby passing it on to Jesus. In fact, Howe admits that the Qumran findings show no evidence of the Essenes ever believing in the doctrine of reincarnation.

Another highly suspect premise in Howe's "Essene-argument" involves his translation and interpretation of Matthew 11:11. Here, he understands "the least" to be "he who is the less [Jesus, the disciple] is greater than he [John the Baptist] in the kingdom of heaven." This view allows Howe to reason that since John the "Essene" believed in reincarnation, Jesus was taught this ancient doctrine and held to it as well.

But the translation of "the least" remains the best translation of the Greek original, for Howe's view would contradict John's claims that Jesus was the greater (Matt. 3:11; John 1:26-34; 3:28-36). The meaning of Matthew 11:11 is that "it is better to enter the kingdom than to herald its coming. John was unique amongst men, but citizenship of the kingdom will be better than his unique position." [11]

Finally, there is no hint of the doctrine of reincarnation in any of the teachings of Jesus. Granting all of Howe's assumptions, it is still implausible to conclude that Jesus was a reincarnationist.

JOHN 3:3

Jesus answered and said to him, "Truly, truly, I say to

you, unless one is born again, he cannot see the kingdom of God."

Must you be born again . . . and again, and again? The
word for *again* has a double reference (common in the book
of John) to "again" and "from above" *(anothen)*. In other
words, John 3:3 refers to both a new birth as well as a
heavenly or spiritual one.

Even though Nicodemus understood "born *anothen*" as
"born a second time" (literally "again" in the same manner), notice that he does so with *sarcasm:* "How can a man
be born when he is old? He cannot enter a second time
into his mother's womb and be born, can he?" (v. 4). The
implication is that Nicodemus found the idea of reincarnation to be absurd and ridiculous.

At this point, Jesus did not affirm that a physical rebirth
was required. Rather, he told Nicodemus, "Unless one is
born of water and the Spirit, he cannot enter into the kingdom of God" (emphasis added). Jesus is speaking here of
a new thing, not the repetition of an old one. *Anothen* is
not to be understood as mere duplication, but in the primary
sense of being born "from above." In fact, everywhere else
in this Gospel *anothen* means "from above" (John 3:31;
19:11).

To be "born from above" is equated in verse 8 with being
"born of the Spirit." This passage is not referring to a
physical rebirth (reincarnation), but a spiritual one (conversion). Further confirmation of a spiritual understanding of
"born again" comes from the rabbinic literature of that
time. The rabbis considered conversion analogous to being
born. "A man's father only brought him into this world;
his teacher, who taught him wisdom, brings him into the
life of the world to come."[12]

Therefore, to be "born again" is best understood in light

of Paul's revelation in 2 Corinthians 5:17: "If any man is in Christ, he is a new creature; the old things passed away; behold, new things have come."

JOHN 9:1-3

> And as He passed by, He saw a man blind from birth. And His disciples asked Him, saying, "Rabbi, who sinned, this man or his parents, that he should be born blind?" Jesus answered, "It was neither that this man sinned, nor his parents; but it was in order that the works of God might be displayed in him."

Reincarnation proponents claim in this passage the disciples assumed reincarnation and that Jesus did nothing to rebuke them for it. For the question as posed, "Rabbi, who sinned, this man or his parents, that he should be born blind?" leads MacGregor to suppose that they entertained two possible explanations:[13]

- His parents or other ancestors had sinned and had transmitted the consequences of their sin to the poor child in the form of congenital blindness.
- The man himself, before his birth, had sinned in some way that had resulted in this terrible misfortune.

The second option implies previous existence. Howe asks, "When could [the blind man] have made such transgressions as to make him blind at birth?" He then reasons that "the only conceivable answer is in some prenatal state." In fact, "the question as posed by the disciples explicitly presupposes prenatal existence."[14] This conclusion is echoed by MacGregor, who insists that "whatever we may take Jesus' own teaching to be on the subject of reincarnation, it is clear that the notion was in the minds of the disciples

144

and of other thoughtful people of the time." This argument is strengthened by the fact that "Christ says nothing to dispel or correct the presupposition." And thus Howe with enthusiasm proclaims,

> Here is incontrovertible support for a doctrine of human preexistence. . . . There is probably no more persuasive passage in the New Testament than this one to support the case that Jesus and his followers accepted or at least were aware of reincarnation.[15]

Howe's excitement is ill-founded. The question posed by the disciples, "Rabbi, who sinned, this man or his parents, that he should be born blind?" does not necessarily mean that the disciples assumed the doctrine of reincarnation. In fact, the historical evidence indicates that the Jewish disciples had something other than reincarnation in mind.

The Jewish theologians of that time gave two reasons for birth defects: pre-natal sin (before birth, but *not before* conception) and parental sin. They claimed that when a pregnant woman worshiped in a heathen temple, the fetus committed idolatry as well. Genesis 25:22 ("the children struggled together within her") was interpreted as a conflict, the result of sin that started from the prenatal stage. It was thought that evil could influence a person from the time of conception. They also believed that the sins of the parents were visited upon the children (Exod. 20:5; Ps. 109:14; Isa. 65:6, 7).[16]

We are not commending these ancient Jewish beliefs in prenatal sin. Rather, these references illustrate that Jewish tradition held to the belief in prenatal sin, *not* reincarnation. And so, it is reasonable to conclude that the disciples assumed such a belief of prenatal sin in accord with their religious tradition which Jesus corrected.

But let's say, for the sake of argument, that the disciples did assume the doctrine of reincarnation. Christ plainly denied it in verse 3 of John 9. For he denied that the blindness had anything to do with the man's sins. Also, the reincarnationist's dependence on some form of karma has no alternative explanation for the cause of the man's blindness.

The reincarnationist understanding of justice demands that birth defects are caused by one's previous sins (see ch. 6). Hence, since Jesus rejects this explanation, the reincarnationist is left without any explanation for this man's blindness. It is absurd to say that Jesus was merely denying the effectual work of karma and rebirth in this *particular case* but not in *principle*. From the karmic perspective, there simply is no other explanation for the defect.

1 CORINTHIANS 15:35-55

> But someone will say, "How are the dead raised? And with what kind of body do they come?" You fool! That which you sow does not come to life unless it dies; and that which you sow, you do not sow the body which is to be, but a bare grain, perhaps of wheat or of something else. But God gives it a body just as He wished, and to each of the seeds a body of its own.

> All flesh is not the same flesh, but there is one flesh of men, and another flesh of beasts, and another flesh of birds, and another of fish. There are also heavenly bodies and earthly bodies, but the glory of the heavenly is one, and the glory of the earthly is another. . . .

> So also is the resurrection of the dead. It is sown a perishable body, it is raised an imperishable body; it is sown in dishonor, it is raised in glory; it is sown in

146

weakness, it is raised in power; it is sown a natural body, it is raised a spiritual body. . . .

The first man is from the earth, earthy; the second man is from heaven. As is the earthy, so also are those who are earthy; and as is the heavenly, so also are those who are heavenly. And just as we have borne the image of the earthy, we shall also bear the image of the heavenly. . . .

Behold, I tell you a mystery; we shall not all sleep, but we shall all be changed, in a moment, in the twinkling of an eye, at the last trumpet; for the trumpet will sound, and the dead will be raised imperishable, and we shall be changed. For this perishable must put on the imperishable, and this mortal must put on immortality. . . .

Then will come about the saying that is written, "Death is swallowed up in victory. O Death, where is your victory? O Death, where is your sting?"

1 Corinthians 15 provides us with perhaps one of the most detailed passages on the nature of our ultimate bodily existence after death. And though this section of Scripture by no means treats the subject of life after death as extensively as we would like, MacGregor believes that Paul provided a clue as to the nature of the resurrection: "each sort of seed gets its own sort of body" (1 Cor. 15:38). This principle, MacGregor says, is very compatible with a reincarnational understanding of human destiny, which does not mean, of course, that Paul taught reincarnationism of the Eastern type.

MacGregor objects to the doctrine of the resurrection that entails "the notion of relinquishing at death the body we now have and assuming another [glorified body] later on." For this body will nevertheless be an "organization that will relate to me as does the present organization of my body . . . relate to me now." Such an understanding "is entirely compatible with any reincarnationist doctrine that is imaginative enough to go beyond the limitations of our present human structure."[17]

MacGregor says the resurrection principle teaches

> that as I grow in grace and am raised by Christ to higher things, the glorified body that is promised me is one that will fit my enhanced state . . . possibly on another planet; but meanwhile, not being ready for that leap, we may pass through some more incarnations in the present type of body, the sort of body to which we are now accustomed.[18]

So then, while the two doctrines of reincarnation and resurrection seem to be incompatible on the surface, "they agree more deeply in their view of man as a psycho-physical [mind-body] unity, so that life after death must be in a body, and a body which expresses the inner character of the individual." In both cases, the person is reembodied. Reincarnationists believe that to be reincarnated is to be resurrected and vice versa. "Thus . . . reincarnation and the resurrection of the body are superficially different but more fundamentally in agreement. For the reincarnation doctrine affirms repeated resurrections of a particular kind."[19]

However, the resurrection should not be confused with reincarnation because the two states are radically different. We have already discussed many types of reincarnation (see ch. 2-3). Now we will look at the biblical doctrine of the resurrection so that we may see its sharp contrast with reincarnation.

The resurrection body of the Lord is the pattern for the resurrection bodies of all the redeemed. Therefore, the best starting place in the study of the nature of the resurrection bodies for the redeemed is with the body of Christ. What is true of Christ's new body will also be true for the new bodies of all the redeemed.[20]

Christ was the first *real* resurrection. When Paul says in 1 Corinthians 15:20 that Christ is "the first fruits [*aparche*] of those who are asleep," he is suggesting both priority in time and superiority in status. Christ became the first of all who will one day come back to life.

Regarding the reincarnationist's attempt to harmonize reincarnation with the resurrection, we find that the nature of reincarnation is fundamentally different from the nature of resurrection. Unlike reincarnation, the resurrected body of Christ could be physically identified as the body he had before his death: he communicated as he did before (Luke 24:13ff.; John 20:11-29; 21:1-23; Acts 1:4-9); his body could be touched (John 20:17, 24-29); and he ate food (Luke 24:42, 43; John 21:1-23).

Yet his resurrected body was different from ordinary physical bodies: he could appear and disappear at will even through closed doors (Luke 24:31; John 20:19, 26), and he ascended into the clouds (Acts 1:9-11).

Snyder admits that the evident change in the Lord's body structure demonstrates that "the resurrection of Jesus Christ was not a simple revivification, the mere return to life of a corpse. . . . His body was raised to a higher level of existence—a level in continuity with, but not limited to, His former bodily form."[21]

Technically speaking, the raisings of Lazarus (John 11:1-44) and of the widow's son (Luke 7:11-17) were *not* resurrections, and no doubt many of the early Christians thought of the resurrection as a revivification of the dead. However, revivification is neither resurrection nor reincarnation.

Paul's concept of the afterlife is one of both continuity and discontinuity (cf. illustration of the seed to plant). In some sense the resurrection body is related to the present, yet, "dimensionally quite a different reality from the present." Paul contrasts the nature of the resurrected body with that of the present earthly body in 1 Corinthians 15:42-44:[22]

Present Body	Resurrected Body
Perishable	Imperishable
Mortal	Immortal
Dishonor	Glory
Weakness	Strength
Earthly	Heavenly
Natural	Supernatural*

All of these contrasts point out the incorruptibility of the resurrection body.

> It will be no longer subject to decay, pain, sickness, or imperfections. The body will be glorious. It will be no longer subject to sin and will be a fit vessel in which to live with God. The body will be powerful. It will no longer have to endure the weakness of old age, or lack of sleep, or sickness. It will then have the power to truly serve God. Finally it will be spiritual. This does not mean that the body lacks real flesh but that it is designed for life in heaven rather than earth.[23]

*See 1 Corinthians 10:4, RSV.

Of course the culminating point of 1 Corinthians 15 is that resurrection denotes the destruction of death, the last enemy. We may now ask the reincarnationist, in what sense can the resurrected body, which cannot die, be identified with the reincarnational body that assumes a perishable nature? For without a perishable nature, one cannot die and be reincarnated. And if the reincarnated state is understood to mean only *one* final transformation rather than *multiple* incarnations, then the doctrine of reincarnation becomes indistinguishable from the traditional resurrection doctrine, and can therefore be discarded.

We can summarize the major differences between resurrection and reincarnation in this way:

Reincarnation	*Resurrection*
Mortal body	Immortal body
Many-times event	One-time event
Intermediate states	Ultimate state
In process	Perfected

Thus, we close the door on reincarnation to be thought of as the ultimate state of resurrection. It does not help the reincarnationist to persist in arguing reincarnation's compatibility with Christianity by relegating the doctrine of rebirth to the traditional notion of the intermediate state either. The intermediate state is the period of being "asleep" in the Lord, awaiting the resurrection of all creation.

A further difference between reincarnation and resurrection is that the former is highly individualistic while the latter is communal. One of the arguments raised by reincarnationists is that reincarnation suits the individual's progression. She moves at her own pace.

For Paul, the resurrection of the dead

> was not an isolated event, not merely the recreation of persons. . . . Rather, it was part and parcel of the creation, . . . Paul's concern is a community of relatedness . . . not a mere grave-emptying operation.[24]

The resurrection of the body is only a part of the new creation of the universe (2 Pet. 3:13). The Christian hope concerns not only my individual fate but the entire creation as well. Because of sin all creation has become involved in death and now waits longingly for deliverance (Rom. 8:19ff.). Like humanity, the world has "fallen." Like humanity, the world "awaits" final judgment and restoration.

This distinctive element of resurrection poses a stark contrast with the doctrine of reincarnation. Even MacGregor admits,

> Wherever such a literalistic understanding [of the Day of Judgment; separation of saved from the lost] prevailed, reincarnation would not fit. Such a literalistic understanding was in fact very common in the first century.[25]

HEBREWS 7:3

> Without father, without mother, without genealogy, having neither beginning of days nor end of life, but made like the Son of God, he [Melchizedek] abides a priest perpetually.

This passage does not teach that Jesus was a reincarnation of Melchizedek as is sometimes taught by reincarnationists. The term "made like" means "resembling." Melchizedek was a "type," a precursor to the future coming Messiah who would also be a priest. The mysterious, unrecorded birth and death of Melchizedek was used as an analogy to the true birthless and deathless, eternal Messiah.

In addition, the context of this passage is a comparison between *priesthoods* rather than *personhoods*. "It is in the timelessness of the priesthood that Melchizedek resembles the Son of God."[26]

JAMES 3:6

> And the tongue is a fire, the very world of iniquity; the tongue is set among our members as that which defiles the entire body, and sets on fire *the course of our life,* and is set on fire by hell (emphasis added).

The phrase "course of our life" can also be translated "wheel of beginnings." This latter translation is sometimes said to be a reference to reincarnation. But the context of the passage indicates that the "wheel of beginnings" refers to the ongoing of life in general, not a continual cycle of beginnings of an individual soul. In the ancient world, the terms "wheel" and "circle" referred to the cycle of the human race (the cycle of successive generations) and the same thought was applied to the whole universe, all parts of which are subject to endless process of formation and decay.

James is not writing about reincarnation. The "wheel of beginnings" or "existence" is used to stress the power and pervasiveness of the human tongue. Here it is used to show the far-reaching effect of the damage that the tongue can do. The context supports this:

> 3:2 A controlled tongue means maturity and a controlled body.
>
> 3:3 A small bit controls the horse.
>
> 3:4 A small rudder controls the whole ship.
>
> 3:5 A small fire puts a whole forest aflame.

3:6 The tongue is a fire which sets aflame the course of human life.

3:7, 8 While man can tame wild beasts, he cannot tame the tongue.

3:9, 10 The same tongue can bless God and curse man.

SUMMARY

None of the verses in Scripture that are used by reincarnationists support the doctrine of reincarnation. Neither do any of the arguments from psychology (ch. 4-5) or justice (ch. 6-8) demonstrate the truth and reality of reincarnation. Reincarnation dogma is not in accord with either right reason or the Scriptures.

We are now in possession of the data needed to refute the so-called "proofs" for reincarnationism. But how do we present this information to our reincarnationist friends or acquaintances? The final chapter deals with the subject of how to witness to a reincarnationist.

HOW TO WITNESS TO A REINCARNATIONIST

Now that we have answered the major arguments for reincarnation, how do we share this knowledge with our reincarnationist neighbor? While this chapter is not exhaustive, it does list some practical ways in which we can become effective defenders of Christian truth as well as helpers to those who are lost in the maze of reincarnationism.[1] This approach centers on three main areas: the prerequisites, the preparation, and the presentation involved in discussing these non-Christian beliefs with a friend.

PREREQUISITES

Nothing is more intimidating to the average Christian than the idea of sharing his faith with someone. Perhaps even more unnerving is the prospect of being involved in what is called "*pre*-evangelism" (*pre*paring the unbeliever for the gospel). Just as evangelism involves "the planting of the seed of the gospel" as well as "reaping the harvest" of converts, pre-evangelism is "the tilling of the soil" of unbelieving hearts. Scripture encourages us to have a firm grasp of the truth so that when people ask us why we believe as we do we will be able to teach them and show those who disagree where they are wrong (1 Pet. 3:15; Titus 1:9).

While some of the content of this book may not have been easy reading, if you have basically understood it up to now, you know enough to defend the Christian hope in the resurrection and to refute the hopeless Eastern teaching of reincarnation. Now, you may say that taking the initiative to discuss reincarnation with a friend "is not natural for me." But as Inter-Varsity national consultant on evangelism Rebecca Manley Pippert has pointed out,

> Actually, the ability to get outside of one's own skin and serve another is not natural for anyone. But sitting back and doing nothing is not an option. We are called to love, to serve, to identify need and to respond. That is not easy for anyone, but it is what the Holy Spirit helps us to do so we can become more like Jesus. Nonetheless, in the way we exercise our love, the way we choose to demonstrate it, the way we share Christ with others we can choose a style comfortable for us.[2]

Pippert's book, *Out of the Salt Shaker and into the World: Evangelism as a Way of Life,* gives clear models of lifestyle evangelism. Just as Jesus discussed spiritual things in a casual way (cf. John 4:1-42, the Samaritan woman), you too can be involved in lifestyle "pre-evangelism" in a comfortable way. You need to realize that through the power of the Holy Spirit (cf. Acts 1:8) and diligent preparation (see next section), God will use you to lead others to the truth of Jesus Christ.

Not only can you discuss the truth of Christianity with people, but you should also realize that people want to hear it. After years of experience in this area, Pippert discovered that we need to see beneath the crust. We must never assume that a person will not be open to Christianity. Again and again I have had to learn that the least likely looking people have been the most open to God.[3]

STRONG SENSE AND CONVICTION OF SALVATION

Motivation for discussing reincarnation with a friend can come from a strong conviction of our own need for salvation, and from the "lostness" of those who need to put their trust in Jesus Christ. The thought of my reincarnationist neighbor potentially being eternally separated from God prompts me to be bolder (yet not offensive) for our Lord. And in a time of relativism where it seems few stand on solid ground, the absolute truth found in Jesus Christ is not only refreshing but respected. Pippert's experience has been that most people respect and respond to a person who communicates clearly rather than apologetically.

BIBLICAL WORLDVIEW

As we have seen from the previous chapter, reincarnation is really just a part of a whole system of beliefs. While there are many different types of reincarnation models (see ch. 2 and 3), the most thorough worldview of reincarnationism is the Eastern one.

When you talk with a reincarnationist, keep in mind that you are essentially dealing with an Eastern, pantheistic worldview. The chart on page 158 is an overview of the likely differences between the Christian's worldview and that of the reincarnationist.[4]

BIBLICAL SUPPORT FOR IMPORTANT DOCTRINES

If you are going to challenge the arguments in favor of reincarnation, you need to be ready to articulate your Chris-

	THEISM *(Judeo-Christian Worldview)*	PANTHEISM *(Eastern Worldview)*
God	One, infinite, personal	One, infinite, impersonal
World	Created out of nothing Finite, temporal	Emanated out of God Eternal
God/ World Relation	God beyond and in the world	God is the world
Miracles	Possible and actual	Impossible
Man's Nature	Soul/body unity Immortalized	Soul/body duality Body mortal/Soul immortal
Man's Immortality	Resurrection of the body	Reincarnation into another body
Man's Ultimate Destiny	Fellowship with God	Merge with God
Jesus Christ	Jesus is the Christ He is the unique God-man	The Christ's spirit was in Jesus; he is merely a man
Atonement	Jesus sacrificially died in our place and provided forgiveness from sin	Jesus was a good example of man perfectly united with God
Sources of Evil	Free choice in this life	Free choices in a past life
End of Evil	Will be defeated by God	Will be reabsorbed into God
Basis of Ethics	Grounded in God	Grounded in lower mani- festations of God
Nature of Ethics	Absolute	Relative
History and It's Goal	Linear, purposeful God appointed end	Circular, illusory endless

tian beliefs. The scriptural defense for Christian beliefs in opposition to reincarnation doctrine is peppered throughout this book. As you learn the arguments against reincarnation, be sure to include the scriptural defense as part of your memory work. In addition, you should have a working knowledge of the basic doctrines of the faith. Two books you may find helpful are Paul E. Little's *Know What You Believe* and *Know Why You Believe.*

ACTIVE PRAYER LIFE

The last but probably most important prerequisite for successfully witnessing to a reincarnationist is an active prayer life. Trying to witness without the Holy Spirit's power and guidance is like trying to drive without gas. Set aside a specific time each day to pray for those to whom you will be witnessing.

PREPARATION

Now that the necessary prerequisites for effective witnessing have been discussed, you need to prepare yourself for the task itself. The material you have read in this book up to this point can help you accomplish the first step in preparing to witness to a reincarnationist.

Begin by building a relationship with your reincarnationist friend. There should be times when reincarnation is not even discussed, like during a stroll in the park or while on a spontaneous outing to the ice cream shop. Show genuine love and concern for the person, who is precious enough in the sight of God to warrant the sacrifice of his Son.

Making an appointment at an appropriate meeting place can set the tone for the conversation. It should be a comfortable place like a coffeehouse where the surroundings are nonthreatening yet secluded from needless distractions. A dormitory lounge or a house where there are kids, television, and ringing telephones could lead to a frustrating experience when trying to carry on any kind of meaningful dialogue.

If possible, go with a Christian friend who can help keep

the conversation from sputtering as well as provide some security for yourself. However, if you choose to take a friend, this should be made clear to the person you are witnessing to. Also, some strategy should be discussed with your partner beforehand.

The key to not being caught off guard is to anticipate some of the questions the reincarnationist might have about Christianity and arguments he might use in favor of reincarnationism. This will prepare you to discuss reincarnationism intelligently. You should have the courage to point out what contradicts the Bible. You do want him to feel your love, but not at the expense of the search for truth.

PRESENTATION

Sooner or later, practice comes to an end, and the "game" must be played. All of the desire, knowledge, and training in the world will not replace the act of witnessing itself. Here are some suggestions for presenting Christian truth in a sensitive manner while refuting non-Christian error:

- Keep a loving attitude.
- Keep the right priorities.
- Ask for his/her testimony on how he/she came to believe in reincarnation.
- Describe your own conversion experience.
- Relate to him/her as a person, not as debating opponent or theologian/scholar.
- Try to stick to central issues.
- Sometimes it is necessary to shake up his/her cult's authority structure.
- End on a personal note.
- Try to meet again.

While the Apostle Peter says "always [be] ready to make a defense to everyone who asks you to give an account for the hope that is in you," he also says that we should do this "with gentleness and reverence" (1 Peter 3:15). Unbelievers should not be seen as targets to gun down. Rather, they are victims to be rescued. Joseph C. Aldrich, author of *Life-style Evangelism*, rightly says,

> Frequently the unsaved are viewed as enemies rather than victims of the Enemy. Spirituality is viewed as separation from the unsaved. The new Christian is told he has "nothing in common" with his unsaved associates. Quite frankly, I have a lot in common with them: a mortgage, car payments, kids who misbehave, a lawn to mow, a car to wash, a less-than-perfect marriage, a few too many pounds around my waist, and an interest in sports, hobbies, and other activities they enjoy. It is well to remember that Jesus was called a "friend of sinners." A *friend* of sinners. Selah![5]

We need to relate to people as people, not as "holier-than-thous." When we present Christian truth alongside the world's falsity, we should not only ask ourselves if we can communicate the content of our message. We should also ask, "Can I go out to dinner with her?" "Can I take him to a ball game?" "Can I invite him over for a game of Scrabble or Trivial Pursuit?" In essence, can we display the love of Christ as well as delineate the truth of Christ? Chuck Swindoll relates this story in his book *Improving Your Serve:*

> A number of years ago, Dr. Waltke, another pastor, a graduate student at Brandeis University (also a semi-

nary graduate), and I toured the mother church of the First Church of Christ Scientist in downtown Boston. The four of us were completely anonymous to the elderly lady who smiled as we entered. She had no idea she was meeting four evangelical ministers—and we chose not to identify ourselves, at least at first.

She showed us several interesting things on the main floor. When we got to the multiple-manual pipe organ, she began to talk about their doctrine and especially their belief about no judgment in the life beyond. Dr. Waltke waited for just the right moment and very casually asked:

"But, Ma'am, doesn't it say somewhere in the Bible, 'It is appointed unto man once to die and after that, the judgment?' " He could have quoted Hebrews 9:27 in Greek! But he was so gracious, so tactful with the little lady. I must confess, I stood back thinking, "Go for it, Bruce. Now we've got her where we want her!"

The lady, without a pause, said simply, "Would you like to see the second floor?"

You know what Dr. Waltke said? "We surely would, thank you."

She smiled, somewhat relieved, and started to lead us up a flight of stairs.

I couldn't believe it! All I could think was, "No, don't let her get away. Make her answer your question!" As I was wrestling within, I pulled on the scholar's arm and said in a low voice, "Hey, why didn't you nail the lady? Why didn't you press the point and not let her get away until she answered?"

Quietly and calmly he put his hand on my shoulder and whispered, "But, Chuck, that wouldn't have been fair. That wouldn't have been very loving, either—now would it?"

Wham! The quiet rebuke left me reeling. I shall *never* forget that moment. And to complete the story, you'll be interested to know that in less than twenty minutes he was sitting with the woman alone, tenderly and carefully speaking with her about the Lord Jesus Christ. She sat in rapt attention. He, the gracious peacemaker, had won a hearing. And I, the scalp-snatcher, had learned an unforgettable lesson.[6]

The first or only Bible many people read may be your life. Have confidence and joy in knowing that you stand on the solid truth of God's Word.

Eventually, the discussion with your friend will need to address the reasons for and against reincarnationism. The best way to get to this point is by asking him *why* he believes *what* he believes. This will not only expose his basis of authority, it can also bring the conversation around to discussing how and why something is true or not. Familiarity with the arguments in this book will greatly help your witnessing strategy.

Most people involved in cults are dependent upon their authority structure or leader (e.g., groups like Bhagwan Shree Rajneesh's, TM, the Unification Church, etc.). This source must be shaken up. Usually criticism of the leader's morals is ineffective. But documented evidence of lies, plagiarism, false prophecy, or cover-ups by the groups' leaders (who are supposedly the sole possessors of truth) can sometimes be very effective. Many competent critiques of various cults and world religions offer specific information of this type.[7]

During discussions when you do not know the answer to a question, you should not "tap dance" around it. It is far more honest to admit ignorance. Express a genuine interest in investigating the possible answers to the question.

One way of discussing reincarnation without having to memorize the contents of this book is to give your friend a copy and work your way through the book together.

Another suggestion is that you use this book as a text for a discussion series at your home. Search Ministries has an excellent program which consists of a series of seven meetings, one a week, for seven weeks. The first three weeks, called the "preliminary meetings," involve Bible study, prayer, and some principles of friendship evangelism for Christians. During the next four weeks non-Christian friends and neighbors are invited to the actual discussion series itself.

Each meeting consists of a "mixer" or party time of snacks, desserts, and even whole meals, along with a discussion lasting no more than an hour. Here is where you can focus in on your friends who believe in reincarnation, Eastern thought, or who are involved in the New Age Movement. The discussion could be led by one leader, by each of the Christians taking turns, or by the whole group, using this book as a basis. The Search home discussion series can serve as an effective way of witnessing to reincarnationists in a friendly and nonconfrontive manner.[8]

Another point to remember is to explain the Christian position in plain language. Just as lawyers, printers, brokers, and others in specialized fields have their own vocabulary, Christian "lingo" is natural for us. To use an analogy, when we have a contract to sign, we have a right to know the meaning of the terms of the document. Likewise, unbelievers have every right to understand the terms of Christianity before they commit themselves to a biblical worldview. Pippert relates this story:

> At an evangelistic dorm talk a non-Christian student asked me, "What does it mean to be a Christian?"

A Christian student who really desired the other student to understand replied, "It means you have to be washed in the blood of the Lamb." The first student paled and looked confused. The Christian continued, "That way you will be sanctified and redeemed."

Another student seeking to help his Christian brother said, "And the fellowship is so neat. Praise the Lord! You really get into the Word and get such a blessing." By the end of the conversation one would have thought these Christians came from another planet.

To the world, evangelical cliches are often either red flags or else the meaning is imprecise. Of course we must not dispense with biblical words or concepts. Instead we need to develop fresh and relevant ways to express what they mean.[9]

We do not mean to convey the idea that evangelism is an easy task. It involves a lot of work and study, courage and stamina, patience and prayer. Yet we are called to do it for the glory of our God and the good of the unsaved. And if there are times of discouragement, remember that whether we "succeed" in convincing someone of the truth of Christianity or not, we are called to be witnesses to our world nonetheless. Our success is being faithful in the *act* of witnessing, not necessarily in the results it may or may not achieve.

Despite the seemingly impossible task of reaching someone holding an Eastern worldview, such a task is not only possible but actual. Like his father before him, Rabi Maharaj was worshiped as a god in India. As a guru, Rabi believed that he was divine and that everything was divine (i.e., pantheism). Reincarnation and karma were accepted along with the rest of Hindu beliefs. And yet, once followed by many and hailed as a god, Rabi Maharaj came to follow the true God, the Father of our Lord Jesus Christ.

How did this devout Hindu who was a practicing yogi from age five turn from his former faith? Through his own honest reasoning he came to realize that reincarnation and other tenets of Hinduism were contrary to clear thinking. And through the bold yet loving witness of a young Christian woman who openly shared the gospel of Christ, Rabi trusted Jesus as his Savior.[10]

People do change their minds. Look around and you will see how many people have turned from their non-Christian beliefs to embrace Christianity. It *can* be done. And *you* could be the instrument God desires to use to help someone turn from his or her belief in reincarnation. No one has said it better than Chuck Swindoll in his excellent book, *Dropping Your Guard:*

> For us to be involved, we must be willing to reach out and risk relating. . . . May I urge you? Risk reaching. Take the initiative. Walk a few feet to your neighbor's yard. Or start with a simple and a warm, sincere wave of the hand. Find some common ground of mutual interest and use that as a basis of conversation. Open up. Be warm and transparent. You may be pleasantly surprised by the results.[11]

A P P E N D I X
REINCARNATION MODELS

MODEL 1: *Hindu "Impersonal" View/Ancient Greek and Roman Views
Hindu "Personal View/Hare Krishna*

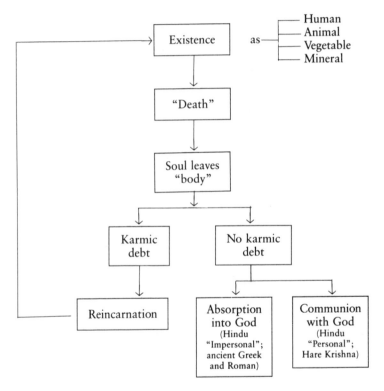

MODEL 2: *Buddhism*

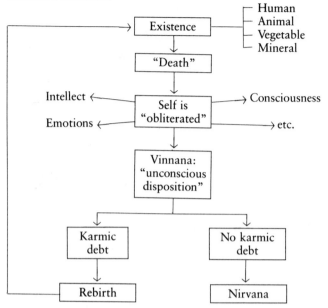

MODEL 3: *Jainism/Sikhism*

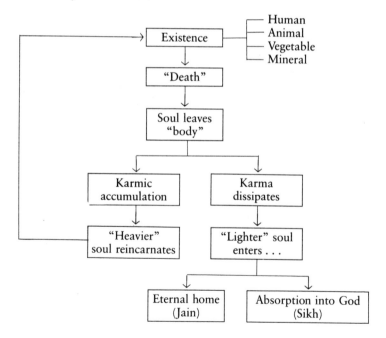

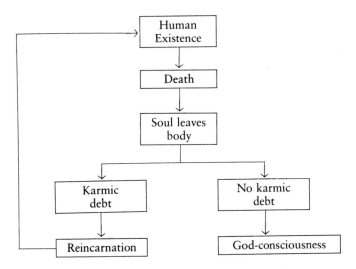

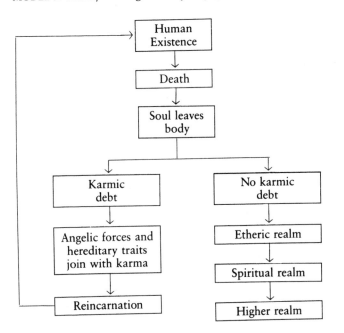

MODEL 6: *Geddes MacGregor*

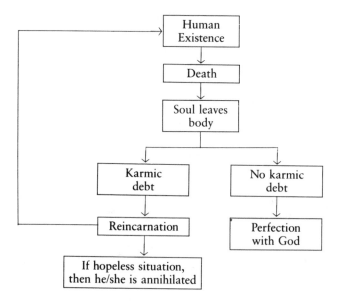

MODEL 7: *Michael Perry, Theory 1*

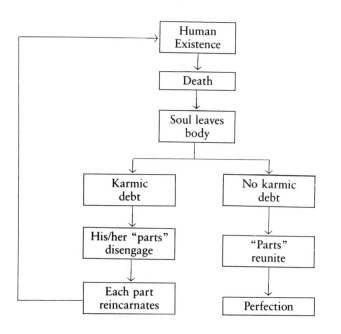

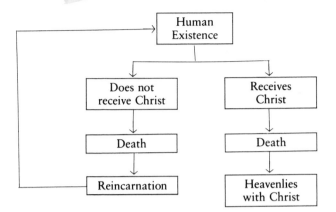

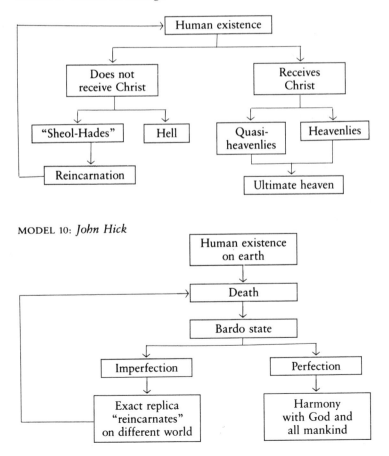

NOTES

CHAPTER 1

[1]Jennifer Boeth, "Reincarnation: A Never-ending Cycle of Lives," *Dallas Times Herald,* 3 April 1983, H1. Based on an actual past-life recall technique of past-life therapist David Yarborough.

[2]George Gallup, Jr., *Adventures in Immortality* (New York: McGraw-Hill, 1982), 192.

[3]*Emerging Trends,* 4:7, September 1982, 3.

[4]Shirley MacLaine, *Out on a Limb* (New York: Bantam Books, 1983), 5.

[5]William A. Henry III, "The Best Year of Her Lives," *Time,* 14 May 1984, 62.

[6]John Leo, "I Was Beheaded in the 1700s," *Time,* 10 September 1984, 68.

[7]"Personalities," *Dallas Times Herald,* 12 May 1983, A2, in *Ladies Home Journal,* June 1983.

[8]Philip Wuntch, "The Singular MacLaine," *Dallas Morning News,* 5 February 1984, C1.

[9]MacLaine, 169.

[10]Leo, 68.

[11]Ibid.

[12]"Anne Francis: A Spiritual Philosophy," *Self-Help Update,* 1984, 24:25.

[13]Maurice S. Rawlings, *Life Wish* (Nashville: Thomas Nelson, 1981), 16-17.

[14]*Self-Help Update,* 1984, 24:3.

[15]Harvey Cox, *Turning East* (New York: Simon & Schuster, 1977), 9.

[16]Os Guinness, *The Dust of Death* (Downers Grove, Ill.: InterVarsity Press, 1973), 195.

[17]John Naisbitt, *Megatrends* (New York: Warner Books, 1982), 240.

[18]Joanne Williams, "Lucas Believes Children Can Learn from Mythology," *Dallas Times Herald,* 25 May 1983, F11.

[19]Dale Pollock, *Skywalking: The Life and Films of George Lucas* (New York: Harmony Books, 1983), 140. See also Norman L. Geisler and J. Yutaka Amano, *Religion of the Force* (Dallas: Quest Publications, 1983) for a more detailed documentation of this point.

[20]Richard de Mille, ed., *The Don Juan Papers* (Santa Barbara, Calif.: Ross-Erickson Pub., 1980), 148-149.

[21]*Update,* 7:4, December 1983, 23.

[22]Gerald B. Derloshon and James B. Potter, *The Success Merchants* (Englewood Cliffs, N.J.: Prentice-Hall, Inc., 1982).

[23]Ibid., 101.

[24]Stanley Doskupil and Brooks Alexander, "Est: The Philosophy of Self-Worship," *SCP Journal,* Winter/1981-1982, 21.

[25]Ibid., 21.

[26]"The Wiz of Show Biz," *Newsweek,* 20 December 1976, 68.

[27]Francis Adeney, "Educators Look East," *SCP Journal,* Winter/1981-1982, 29-31.

[28]Marilyn Ferguson, *The Aquarian Conspiracy* (Los Angeles: J. P. Tarcher, 1980), 23.

[29]Mark Satin, *New Age Politics* (New York: Dell Pub., 1978), 7-8.

[30]Robert Muller, *New Genesis: Shaping a Global Spirituality* (New York: Doubleday, 1982), dedication page.

[31]John H. Hick, *Death and Eternal Life* (New York: Harper & Row, 1976), 89.

[32]Ibid., 90.

[33]Ibid.

[34]Boeth, H1.

CHAPTER 2

[1]Geoffrey Parrinder, *Dictionary of Non-Christian Religions* (Philadelphia: Westminster Press, 1971), 286.

[2]John H. Hick, *Death and Eternal Life* (New York: Harper & Row, 1976), 311.

[3]See Norman L. Geisler and William D. Watkins's *Perspectives: Understanding and Evaluating Today's World Views* (San Bernardino, Calif.: Here's Life Pubs., 1984), ch. 4.

[4]Hick claims that Ramanuja's system is theistic, presumably because Ramanuja held that God is personal *(Death and Eternal Life,* ch. 17). However, theism holds to a radical distinction between God and the world, between the Creator and creation (see Geisler and Watkins's *Perspectives,* ch. 2).

[5]Hick, *Death,* 315.

[6]Parrinder, 151.

[7]Ibid.

[8]John B. Noss, *Man's Religions,* 6th ed. (New York: MacMillan, 1980), 90.

[9]John H. Hick, "Reincarnation," in *The Westminster Dictionary of Christian Theology* (Philadelphia: Westminster Press, 1983), 491.

[10]Ninian Smart, "Reincarnation," in *Encyclopedia of Philosophy,* (New York: MacMillan, 1972), 7:122; Noss, 90.

[11]K. M. Sen, *Hinduism* (New York: Penguin, 1962), 23.

[12]Hick, *Death,* 428.

[13]"The Buddha did teach that there was no self or ego as we know it in the final nirvana; but he did not deny the saint's existence" (L. Stafford Betty, "Personal Survival in the World's Scriptures: Its Relevance for the Modern Inquirer," *Journal of Religion and Psychical Research,* January 1982, 8). Likewise, David J. Kaluapahana in *Buddhist Philosophy: A Historical Analysis* says that the "denial of identity does not imply denial of continuity" (Honolulu: University Press of Hawaii, 1976).

[14]Hick, *Death,* 344.

[15]Smart, "Reincarnation," 7:123.

[16]W. Y. Evans-Wentz, ed., *The Tibetan Book of the Dead* (New York: Oxford University Press, 1960), 43.

[17]Ninian Smart, "Nirvana," in *Encyclopedia of Philosophy* (New York: MacMillan, 1972), 5:518.

[18]Ninian Smart, "Jainism," in *Encyclopedia of Philosophy* (New York: MacMillan, 1972), 4:238; Noss, 98-100; Stuart C. Hackett, *Oriental Philosophy* (Madison: University of Wisconsin Press, 1979), 190.

[19]Noss, 223-224.

[20]A. C. Bhaktivedanta Swami Prabhupada, *Coming Back: The Science of Reincarnation* (Los Angeles: The Bhaktivedanta Book Trust, 1982), 16, 33.

[21]Ibid., 122-123.

[22]Ibid.

CHAPTER 3

[1]1969 Gallup Poll cited in Mark Albrecht, *Reincarnation: A Christian Appraisal* (Downers Grove, Ill.: InterVarsity Press, 1982), 12.

[2]John B. Noss, *Man's Religions*, 6th ed. (New York: MacMillan, 1980), 52.

[3]William R. Inge, *The Philosophy of Plotinus,* 3d ed. (1929; reprint, New York: Greenwood Press, 1968), 2:33; cf. 3.4.6; 4.8.5. It should be noted that there is some debate whether or not Plotinus took the doctrine of reincarnation very seriously because he is inconsistent in regard to the nature of the re-embodiment in terms of retributive justice.

[4]Plotinus, "The Six Enneads," in *Great Books of the Western World,* vol. 17, trans. Stephen MacKenna, ed. B. S. Page (Chicago: Encyclopedia Britannica, 1952), 3.4.2.

[5]Inge, 2:33.

[6]Innocent C. Onyewuenyi, "A Philosophical Reappraisal of African Belief in Reincarnation," *International Philosophical Quarterly,* September 1982, 166.

[7]Irving S. Cooper, *Reincarnation: A Hope of the World* (Wheaton, Ill.: Theosophical Pub. House, 1979), 25.

[8]Manly P. Hall, *Reincarnation: The Cycle of Necessity* (Los Angeles: Philosophical Research Society, 1967), 20; see also G. de Purucker, *Studies in Occult Philosophy* (Pasadena: Theosophical University Press, 1973), 350, 356.

[9]de Purucker, 472.

[10]Ibid., 356.

[11]Alice Bailey, *The Reappearance of the Christ* (New York: Lucis, 1978), 119.

[12]de Purucker, 301.

[13]Phillip J. Swihart, *Reincarnation, Edgar Cayce and the Bible* (Downers Grove, Ill.: InterVarsity Press, 1975), 16.

[14]I. E. Sharma, *Cayce, Karma and Reincarnation* (Wheaton, Ill.: Theosophical Pub. House, 1975), 85.

[15]"Interview: Lynn Sparrow," in *Update,* March 1983, 21. Lynn Sparrow is manager at the Virginia Beach-based Association for Research and Enlightenment, Inc. (ARE), a worldwide nonprofit membership organization founded in 1931 by the late psychic Edgar Cayce.

[16]Sharma, 91.

[17]Quincy Howe, Jr., *Reincarnation for the Christian* (Philadelphia: Westminster press, 1974), 20, 22.

[18]Ibid., 36.

[19]Ibid., 31-32.

[20]Ibid., 100.

[21]Ibid., 22.

[22]Hugo H. Culpepper, untitled review, *Review and Expositor,* Winter 1975, 121.

[23]Frederick A. M. Spencer, *The Future Life: A New Interpretation of the Christian Doctrine* (New York: Harper & Row, 1935), 297.

[24]Ibid., 304, 307.

[25]Rudolf Frieling, *Christianity and Reincarnation,* trans. Rudolf and Margaret Koehler (Edinburgh: Floris Books, 1977), 114-116.

[26]Ibid., 66.

[27]Ibid., 90.

[28]Geddes MacGregor, *Reincarnation as a Christian Hope* (Totowa, N. J.: Barnes & Noble Imports, 1982), ix.

[29]Geddes MacGregor, *Reincarnation in Christianity* (Wheaton, Ill.: Theosophical Pub. House, 1978), 7; see also MacGregor, *Christian Hope,* 1x.

[30]MacGregor, *Christianity,* 19-20.

[31]Geddes MacGregor, *The Christening of Karma: The Secret of Evolution* (Wheaton, Ill.: Theosophical Pub. House, 1984), 8-9.

[32]MacGregor, *Christianity,* 2.

[33]Ibid., 3; see also MacGregor, *Christian Hope,* 28.

[34]Ibid., 171.

[35]Ibid., 167-168.

[36]Michael Perry, *Psychic Studies: A Christian's View* (Wellingborough, Northamptonshire: The Aquarian Press, 1984), 187.

[37]Ibid., 186.

[38]Ibid., 187.

[39]Ibid., 213.

[40]John J. Hearney. *The Sacred and the Psychic: Parapsychology and Christian Theology* (New York: Paulist Press, 1984), 217.

[41]William L. de Arteaga, *Past Life Visions: A Christian Exploration* (New York: Seabury Press, 1983), 207-208.

[42]Ibid., 207-209.

[43]John H. Hick, *Death and Eternal Life* (New York: Harper & Row, 1976), 203.

[44]Ibid., 279-285.

[45]Stephen H. Travis, *Christian Hope and the Future* (Downers Grove, Ill.: InterVarsity Press, 1980), 102; see also Hick, *Death,* 289-295.

[46]John H. Hick, "Present and Future Life," *Harvard Theological Review,* January-April 1978, 12.

[47]Hick, *Death,* 13.

[48]Ibid., 419.

[49]Hick, "Future Life," 13.

[50]Hick, *Death,* 455.

CHAPTER 4

[1]Ian Stevenson, "The Explanatory Value of the Idea of Reincarnation," *The Journal of Nervous and Mental Disease,* September 1977, 305.

[2]Jennifer Boeth, "In Search of Past Lives: Looking at Yesterday to Find Answers for Today," *Dallas Times Herald,* 3 April 1983, H1.

[3]Ibid., H3.

[4]Ibid., H1.

[5] William L. de Arteaga, *Past Life Visions: A Christian Exploration* (New York: Seabury Press, 1983), 153-163.

[6] Martin and Diedre Bobgan, *Hypnosis and the Christian* (Minneapolis: Bethany House, 1984), 46.

[7] Boeth, "In Search," H1, 3.

[8] John H. Hick, *Death and Eternal Life* (New York: Harper & Row, 1976), 373-374; see also Louisa E. Rhine, "Review of Ian Stevenson, Twenty Cases Suggestive of Reincarnation," *The Journal of Parapsychology,* December 1966, 265.

[9] Stevenson, 325.

[10] Boeth, "In Search," H3.

[11] Walter Martin, *The Riddle of Reincarnation* (Santa Ana, Calif.: Vision House, 1977), 18.

[12] Bobgan, 15.

[13] John S. Gillis, "The Therapist as Manipulator," *Psychology Today,* December 1974, 91.

[14] Bobgan, 35.

[15] Stevenson, 310.

[16] Bernard L. Diamond, "Inherent Problems in the Use of Pretrial Hypnosis on a Prospective Witness," *California Law Review,* March 1980, 333-337.

[17] Elizabeth Stark, "Hypnosis on Trial," *Psychology Today,* February 1984, 35.

[18] Ibid.

[19] Bobgan, 25; "State Supreme Court Rejects Hypnosis Testimony," *Santa Barbara News Press,* 12 March 1982, A16; see also Diamond, 333-337.

[20] Stark, 36.

[21] Bobgan, 28-29; Charles Tart, "Measuring Hypnotic Depth," *Hypnosis: Developments in Research and New Perspectives,* Erika Fromm and Ronald Shorr, eds. (New York: Aldine Pub. Co., 1979), 594.

[22] Tart, 596.

[23] Bobgan, 31-32; William Kroger, *Clinical and Experimental Hypnosis,* 2d ed. (Philadelphia: J. B. Lippincott, 1977), 126.

[24] E. D. Walker, *Reincarnation: A Study of Forgotten Truth* (New York: University Books, 1965), 49, 51.

CHAPTER 5

[1] Harold Rosen, *A Scientific Report on "The Search for Bridey Murphy"* (New York: Julian Press, 1956); Martin Gardner, *Fads and Fallacies* (New York: Dover Pub., 1974).

[2] Maurice S. Rawlings, *Life Wish* (Nashville: Thomas Nelson, 1981), 103.

[3] C. T. K. Chari, "Some Critical Considerations concerning Karma and Rebirth," in *Indian Philosophical Annual,* 1965, 132-133.

[4] Ian Stevenson, "The Explanatory Value of the Idea of Reincarnation," *The Journal of Nervous and Mental Disease,* September 1977, 308.

[5] William L. de Arteaga, *Past Life Visions: A Christian Exploration* (New York: Seabury Press, 1983), 111-112.

[6] Thomas Sugue, *The Story of Edgar Cayce: There Is a River,* rev. ed. (Virginia Beach: Association for Research and Enlightenment, 1973), 210.

[7] Lynn A. de Silva, *Reincarnation in Buddhist and Christian Thought* (Columbo: Christian Literature Society, 1968), 70.

[8] de Arteaga, 174.

[9] Frances Adeney, "Hope in Reincarnation: Elisabeth Kubler-Ross and Life after Death," *SCP Journal,* August-September 1982, 3.

[10]Jesse Kornbluth, "The Fuehrer over Est," *New Times,* 19 March 1976, 42.

[11]Brad Steiger, *You Will Live Again* (New York: Dell, 1978), 205-206.

[12]Jennifer Boeth, "In Search of Past Lives: Looking at Yesterday to Find Answers for Today," *Dallas Times Herald,* 3 April 1983, H1.

[13]Shirley MacLaine, *Out on a Limb* (New York: Bantam Books, 1983), 199.

CHAPTER 6

[1]Quincy Howe, Jr., *Reincarnation for the Christian* (Philadelphia: Westminster Press, 1974), 51.

[2]John H. Hick, *Death and Eternal Life* (New York: Harper & Row, 1976), 200-201.

[3]Howe, 53.

[4]Frederick A. M. Spencer, *The Future Life: A New Interpretation of the Christian Doctrine* (New York: Harper & Row, 1935), 303-304.

[5]Hick, *Death,* 247.

[6]Lynn A. de Silva, *Reincarnation in Buddhist and Christian Thought* (Columbo: Christian Literature Society, 1968), 147.

[7]Hick, *Death,* 259.

[8]Geddes MacGregor, *Reincarnation as a Christian Hope* (Totowa, N.J.: Barnes & Noble Imports, 1982), 11.

[9]Geddes MacGregor, *Reincarnation in Christianity* (Wheaton, Ill.: Theosophical Pub. House, 1978), 171.

[10]William L. de Arteaga, *Past Life Visions: A Christian Exploration* (New York: Seabury Press, 1983), 215-216.

[11]de Silva, 154.

[12]MacGregor, *Christianity,* 19.

[13]MacGregor, *Christian Hope,* 141.

[14]Hick, *Death,* 239, 210.

[15]Howe, 32.

[16]MacGregor, *Christian Hope,* 28.

[17]Geddes MacGregor, *The Christening of Karma* (Wheaton, Ill.: Theosophical Pub. House, 1984), 61, 63.

[18]E. D. Walker, *Reincarnation: A Study of Forgotten Truth* (New York: University Books, 1965), 32.

[19]John King-Farlow, "Scepticism, Evil, and Original Sin: A Case for Reincarnation?" in *The Challenge of Religion Today: Essays on the Philosophy of Religion* (New York: Science History Pub., 1976), 39.

[20]Geddes MacGregor, "The Christening of Karma," in *Karma: The Universal Law of Harmony,* ed. Virginia Hanson and Rosemarie Stewart (Wheaton, Ill.: Theosophical Pub. House, 1975), 4.

[21]Howe, 107.

[22]Walker, 285.

[23]MacGregor, *Christianity,* 168.

[24]MacGregor, "The Christening," 3.

CHAPTER 7

[1]Leon Nemoy, "Biblical Quasi-evidence for the Transmigration of Souls," *Journal of Biblical Literature,* 1940, 162.

[2]Mark Albrecht, *Reincarnation: A Christian Appraisal* (Downers Grove, Ill.: InterVarsity Press, 1982), 108.

[3]John H. Hick, untitled review, *Religion,* Autumn 1975, 175.

[4]See Paul J. Griffiths's excellent article, "Notes towards a Critique of Buddhist Karmic Theory," in *Religious Studies,* September 1983, 277-291.

[5]Norman L. Geisler, *Roots of Evil* (Grand Rapids: Zondervan, 1978), 37; see also Alvin C. Plantinga's *God, Freedom, and Evil* (Grand Rapids: Eerdmans, 1974).

[6]John H. Hick, *Evil and the God of Love*, rev. ed. (New York: Harper & Row, 1978), 341.

[7]Gerhard von Rad, *Wisdom in Israel*, trans. James D. Martin (Nashville: Abingdon Press, 1972), 124-137.

[8]Robert Gordis, *The Book of Job* (New York: Jewish Theological Seminary of America, 1978), xxx.

[9]Christopher J. H. Wright, *An Eye for an Eye: The Place of Old Testament Ethics Today* (Downers Grove, Ill.: InterVarsity Press, 1983), 166.

[10]John Snyder, *Reincarnation vs. Resurrection* (Chicago: Moody Press, 1984), 88.

[11]William L. de Arteaga, *Past Life Visions: A Christian Exploration* (New York: Seabury Press, 1983), 81.

[12]Albrecht, 93.

[13]Kana Mitra, "Human Rights in Hinduism," in *Journal of Ecumenical Studies*, Summer 1982, 84.

[14]Loren Eisley, *The Immense Journey* (New York: Random House, 1957), 199.

[15]Colin Patterson, "Evolutionism and Creationism," speech given at the American Museum of Natural History, New York, 5 November 1981.

[16]Geddes MacGregor, *Reincarnation as a Christian Hope* (Totowa, N.J.: Barnes & Noble Imports, 1982), 72.

[17]Stephen H. Travis, *Christian Hope and the Future* (Downers Grove, Ill.: InterVarsity Press, 1980), 131.

CHAPTER 8

[1]We are indebted for the following argument to S. Craig Glickman, "The Nature of the Atonement" (unpublished class notes in Soteriology, Dallas Theological Seminary, Fall 1983), 19-21.

[2]William G. T. Shedd, *Dogmatic Theology*, 2d ed. (Nashville: Thomas Nelson, 1980), 2:382-383.

[3]Robert A. Morey, *Death and the Afterlife* (Minneapolis: Bethany House, 1984), 12.

[4]Norman L. Geisler, *Options in Contemporary Christian Ethics* (Grand Rapids: Baker Book House, 1981), 95.

[5]Ibid., 89.

[6]Manly Hall, *Reincarnation: The Cycle of Necessity* (Los Angeles: Philosophical Research Society, 1967), 183, 185.

[7]Geddes MacGregor, *Reincarnation as a Christian Hope* (Totowa, N.J.: Barnes & Noble Imports, 1982), 136.

[8]Quincy Howe, Jr., *Reincarnation for the Christian* (Philadelphia: Westminster Press, 1974), 52.

[9]MacGregor, *Christian Hope*, 30.

[10]John Snyder, *Reincarnation vs. Resurrection* (Chicago: Moody Press, 1984), 59-60.

[11]John J. Hearney, *The Sacred and the Psychic: Parapsychology and Christian Theology* (New York: Paulist Press, 1984), 218.

[12]William L. de Arteaga, *Past Life Visions: A Christian Exploration* (New York: Seabury Press, 1983), 79.

[13]Morey, 233.

[14]John H. Hick, *Death and Eternal Life* (New York: Harper & Row, 1976), 249.
[15]Paul Helm, "Universalism and the Threat of Hell," *Trinity Journal*, Spring 1983, 35-43.
[16]Ibid., 42.
[17]Shedd, 2:676.
[18]Helm, 43.
[19]Shedd, 2:715.
[20]J. Kerby Anderson, *Life, Death and Beyond* (Grand Rapids: Zondervan, 1980), 167.
[21]Norman L. Geisler, *Roots of Evil* (Grand Rapids: Zondervan, 1978), 61.
[22]Hick, *Death*, 251.
[23]See Norman L. Geisler, "Man's Destiny: Free or Forced?" in *Christian Scholar Review* 9, 1979, 99-109; see also Geisler's "Responses to My Critics," in *Christian Scholar Review* 9, 1979, 116-120.
[24]Geddes MacGregor, *Reincarnation in Christianity* (Wheaton, Ill.: Theosophical Pub. House, 1978), 160.
[25]MacGregor, *Christian Hope*, 146.
[26]Shedd, 2:722.
[27]Ibid., 2:741.
[28]Nicolas Berdiaev, *Truth and Revelation*, 146-147.
[29]John Wenham, *The Goodness of God* (Downers Grove, Ill.: InterVarsity Press, 1974), 34.
[30]Snyder, 82.

CHAPTER 9
[1]Geddes MacGregor, *Reincarnation as a Christian Hope* (Totowa, N.J.: Barnes & Noble Imports, 1982), 42.
[2]John A. Thompson, *The Book of Jeremiah* of the *New International Commentary on the Old Testament Series* (Grand Rapids): Eerdmans, 1980), 145.
[3]William L. de Arteaga, *Past Life Visions: A Christian Exploration* (New York: Seabury Press, 1983), 123.
[4]Quincy Howe, Jr., *Reincarnation for the Christian* (Philadelphia: Westminster Press, 1974), 96.
[5]Ibid., 88-90.
[6]Ibid., 91.
[7]Ibid.
[8]Josephus, *Antiquities of the Jews*, 9.2.2.
[9]Walter Kaiser, "The Promise of the Arrival of Elijah in Malachi and the Gospels," in *Grace Theological Journal*, Fall 1982, 221-233.
[10]F. F. Bruce, *New Testament History* (Garden City, N.Y.: Doubleday, 1969), 152-162.
[11]Willoughby C. Allen, *The Gospel According to St. Matthew*, 3d ed., of *The International Critical Commentary* (Edinburgh: T & T Clark, 1972), 115.
[12]J. H. Bernard, *A Critical and Exegetical Commentary on the Gospel According to St. John*, 2 vols., of *The International Critical Commentary* (Edinburgh: T & T Clark, 1963), 1:clxiii.
[13]MacGregor, *Christian Hope*, 43.
[14]Howe, 93.
[15]Ibid., 93-94; see also MacGregor, *Christian Hope*, 43, and de Arteaga, 198.

[16]Herman L. Strack and Paul Billerbeck, *Kommentar zum New Testament aus Talmud und Midrash,* 2:527-529.

[17]MacGregor, *Christian Hope,* 9.

[18]Ibid., 40.

[19]John H. Hick, *Death and Eternal Life* (New York: Harper & Row, 1976), 371-372.

[20]Edward Wayne Brooks, "The Nature of the Resurrection Body" (Th.M. thesis, Dallas Theological Seminary, May 1971), 36.

[21]John Snyder, *Reincarnation vs. Resurrection* (Chicago: Moody Press, 1984), 61.

[22]Gerald L. Borchert, "The Resurrection: 1 Corinthians 15," in *Review and Expositor,* Summer 1983, 411.

[23]Brooks, 49-50.

[24]Lloyd R. Bailey, Sr., *Biblical Perspectives on Death* (Philadelphia: Fortress Press, 1979), 90.

[25]MacGregor, *Christian Hope,* 7-8.

[26]Thomas Hewitt, *The Epistle to the Hebrews: An Introduction and Commentary* (Grand Rapids: Eerdmans, 1961), 117.

CHAPTER 10

[1]The overall outline of this chapter has been adapted from Eric Pement's article "Witnessing to Cults," in *SCP Journal* 9:5, November-December 1983, 9-10.

[2]Rebecca Manley Pippert, *Out of the Salt Shaker and into the World: Evangelism as a Way of Life* (Downers Grove, Ill.: InterVarsity Press, 1979), 123-124.

[3]Ibid., 115-116.

[4]This chart is based on Norman L. Geisler and William Watkins's *Perspectives: Understanding and Evaluating Today's World Views* (San Bernardino, Calif.: Here's Life Pubs., 1984), 244-245.

[5]Joseph C. Aldrich, *Life-style Evangelism: Crossing Traditional Boundaries to Reach the Unbelieving World* (Portland, Oreg.: Multnomah, 1981), 20.

[6]Chuck Swindoll, *Improving Your Serve: The Art of Unselfish Living* (Waco, Tex.: Word, 1981), 119-120.

[7]See Kenneth Boa, *Cults, World Religions, and You;* Ronald Enroth et al., *A Guide to Cults and New Religions;* Walter Martin, *The Kingdom of the Cults* and *The New Cults;* Josh McDowell and Don Stewart, *Handbook of Today's Religions;* Bob Larson, *Larson's Book of Cults;* and Robert and Gretchen Passantino, *Answers to the Cultist at Your Door.*

[8]Write Search Ministries, Inc., National Office, P. O. Box 521, Lutherville, MD 21093. Telephone: (301) 252-1246.

[9]Pippert, 130-131.

[10]Rabindranath R. Maharaj and Dave Hunt, *Death of a Guru,* ed. Russell Hitt (Nashville: Holman, 1977), 104. See also Rabindranath Maharaj, "Rebirth of a Yogi: Rabi Maharaj's Story," pamphlet by Spiritual Counterfeits Project, Box 2418, Berkeley, CA 94702.

[11]Chuck Swindoll, *Dropping Your Guard* (Waco, Tex.: Word, 1983), 76.

GLOSSARY

Brahman. In Hinduism, it denotes the principal and ultimate reality which is identical with all that is (cf. *Pantheism*).

Hypnotherapy. A psychological therapy which involves the use of hypnosis.

Hypnotic Regression. The process by which one is said to recall past-life memories through hypnosis.

Jiva, Jivatman. Commonly translated and understood as referring to what Westerners call the "soul"—that individual agent which endures throughout one's reincarnations.

Karma. The law of cause and effect which says that for every action (in this life) there is a reaction (in the next life). What we sow in this life we will reap in the next life.

Metempsychosis. Ancient Greek word which essentially means the same thing as reincarnation.

Moksha. The final state of "deliverance" from the burdensome cycle of reincarnation.

Nirvana. Literally, "cessation" or "extinction"; this term is interpreted in a variety of ways in Buddhism. But it minimally means the cessation from being trapped in the wheel of rebirth and selfish craving.

Pantheism. The worldview which holds that all is God and God is all. There is no difference between God and the world.

Parapsychology. The field of scientific study which purports to examine phenomena which cannot be explained by conventional theories of psychology.

Rebirth. Technically, this differs from reincarnation in that the individual who dies is not reborn as the same self.

Reincarnation. The belief that the soul after death passes on to another body.

Retrocognition. The process of knowing past information which is usually attained through some paranormal methods.

Samsara. The continual cycle of rebirth.

Spontaneous Past-Life Recall. The process by which one is said to remember his/her past life without artificially induced means (i.e., hypnosis).

Theism. The worldview which holds that God is the cause and sustainer of the world. God and the world are not regarded as being identical with each other. God is beyond the world as well as active in it.

Transmigration. The movement of the soul from one body to another. Transmigration is commonly used as broadly referring to the reincarnations of many different types of life-forms, such as mineral, vegetative, and animal, as well as human.

Vinnana. In Buddhism, it is the "unconscious disposition" of the deceased which is reborn. It is not to be confused with the conscious self, soul, mind, etc.

S E L E C T E D
B I B L I O G R A P H Y

BOOKS FAVORING REINCARNATION

de Arteaga, William L. *Past Life Visions: A Christian Exploration*. New York: Seabury Press, 1983.

Evans-Wentz, W. Y., ed. *The Tibetan Book of the Dead*. New York: Oxford University Press, 1960.

Frieling, Rudolf. *Christianity and Reincarnation*. Translated by Rudolf and Margaret Koehler. Edinburgh: Floris Books, 1977.

Hall, Manly P. *Reincarnation: The Cycle of Necessity*. Los Angeles: Philosophical Research Society, Inc., 1939, 1967.

Hanson, Virginia and Rosemarie Stewart, eds. *Karma: The Universal Law of Harmony*. Wheaton, Ill.: Theosophical Pub. House, 1975.

Head, J. and S. L. Cranston. *Reincarnation: An East-West Anthology*. Wheaton, Ill.: Theosophical Pub. House, 1961.

———. *Reincarnation in World Thought*. New York: Julian Press, 1967.

———. *Reincarnation: The Phoenix Fire Mystery*. New York: Warner Books, 1979.

Hearney, John J. *The Sacred and the Psychic: Parapsychology and Christian Theology*. New York: Paulist Press, 1984.

Hick, John H. *Death and Eternal Life*. New York: Harper & Row, 1976.

———. *Evil and the God of Love*. Rev. ed. New York: Harper & Row, 1978.

Howe, Jr., Quincy. *Reincarnation for the Christian*. Philadelphia: Westminster Press, 1974.

Kalupahana, David J. *Buddhist Philosophy: A Historical Analysis*. Honolulu: University Press of Hawaii, 1976.

King-Farlow, John. "Scepticism, Evil and Original Sin." In *The Challenge of Religion Today: Essays on the Philosophy of Religion,* edited by John King-Farlow, 26-42. New York: Science History Pub., 1976.

MacGregor, Geddes. *The Christening of Karma: The Secret of Evolution*. Wheaton, Ill.: Theosophical Pub. House, 1984.

———. *Reincarnation as a Christian Hope*. Totowa, N.J.: Barnes & Noble Imports, 1982.

185

————. *Reincarnation in Christianity*. Wheaton, Ill.: Quest Books, 1978.

MacLaine, Shirley. *Out on a Limb*. New York: Bantam Books, 1983.

Perry, Michael. *Psychic Studies: A Christian's View*. Wellingborough, Northamptonshire: The Aquarian Press, 1984.

Radhakrishnan, Sarvepalli. *East and West: Some Reflections*. London: George Allen and Unwin, 1955.

————. *Eastern Religions and Western Thought*. London: Oxford University Press, 1939.

Radhakrishnan, Sarvepalli and Charles A. Moore, eds. *A Sourcebook in Indian Philosophy*. Princeton: Princeton University Press, 1957.

Spencer, Frederick A. M. *The Future Life: A New Interpretation of the Christian Doctrine*. New York: Harper & Row, 1935.

Stevenson, Ian. *Twenty Cases Suggestive of Reincarnation*. Charlottesville, Va.: University Press of Virginia, 1966.

Walker, E. D. *Reincarnation: A Study of Forgotten Truth*. New Hyde Park, N.Y.: University Books, 1965.

BOOKS EVALUATING REINCARNATION

Albrecht, Mark. *Reincarnation: A Christian Appraisal*. Downers Grove, Ill.: InterVarsity Press, 1982.

Anderson, J. Kerby, *Life, Death and Beyond*. Grand Rapids, Mich.: Zondervan Publishing House, 1980.

de Silva, Lynn A. *Reincarnation in Buddhist and Christian Thought*. Columbo: Christian Literature Society, 1968.

Hackett, Stuart C. *Oriental Philosophy: A Westerner's Guide to Eastern Thought*. Madison: University of Wisconsin Press, 1979.

Martin, Walter R. *The Riddle of Reincarnation*. Santa Ana, Calif.: Vision House Publishers, 1977.

Morey, Robert A. *Death and the Afterlife*. Minneapolis: Bethany House, 1984.

————. *Reincarnation and Christianity*. Minneapolis: Bethany House, 1980.

Naipaul, V. S. *An Area of Darkness*. New York: Random House, 1964.

————. *India: A Wounded Civilization*. New York: Random House, 1976, 1977.

Snyder, John. *Reincarnation vs. Resurrection*. Chicago: Moody Press, 1984.

Travis, Stephen H. *Christian Hope and the Future*. Downers Grove, Ill.: InterVarsity Press, 1980.